Text Copyright © 2019 Seattle

Copyright ©2019 Oakes Books Publisher

All rights reserved, no part of this book, either text or illustration, may be used or

reproduced in any form without prior written permission from the publisher.

Eleven Principles for Living is published by Oakes Publishing, oneoakes@gmail.com. Copyrights © 2019 by Oakes Books and Robert L Jeffrey Ministries, Seattle, Washington 98122. Printed and distributed in the United States, by Lightning Source. Scriptures taken from the *King James Version* and *English Standard Version*. Lessons and/or readings based on Reverend Dr. Robert L Jeffrey Studies.

Graphic Art Design by Scribes Freelance

Dear Readers

Thank you for participating in this faith journey. This workbook is the first in a series of books exploring the Christian message to the 'Now' generation. This is the generation that has to deal with the prevailing issues of today; such as the national epidemic of youth violence, police brutality, racism, government upheaval, changing social attitudes about sexuality, changing role of women in society and in the church, rising importance of technology, just to name a few issues to be covered in this series.

It is the intent of this series to help you to better understand the message of the ancient text, and how it fits into the context of your everyday life. I have been a pastor for over 50 years, and in that time, I have always sought to make the bible relevant to the current times we live in.

In this series we will deal with every problem and situation that, at one time or another, many of you will face. For example, we also will deal with the problems of anxiety and failure that can lead to addictions. This series will seek to guide you biblically to an enlightened understanding of where the Kingdom of God on earth should be on these issues facing our modern world.

There will be times during our journey together when you will have questions concerning some of the conclusions that we will reach. That will be fine. These books are not the bible, neither are they infallible. They are simply an expression of what the Holy Spirit has revealed to me, as I have attempted to be the best minister that I could be during my 50 years of service to the Kingdom of God.

Therefore; I welcome you to journey with me as we seek together, to speak to these times using the word of God as our guide.

Sincerely,

Dr. Robert L. Jeffrey, Sr.

Table of Contents

1st Principle	Page
Give God the Glory	7
2nd Principle	
Keep A Positive Attitude	19
3rd Principle	
Appreciate What You Have	27
4th Principle	
Stay Woke	36
5th Principle	
The Power of Investment	46
6th Principle	
Accepting Leadership Responsibility	59

Table of Contents

(Continue)

Maps	Page
The Twelve Tribes of Israel	68
King David's Empire	69
Path of the Ancient Hebrews	70

7th Principle
Use Failure As A Stepping-Stone 71

8TH Principle
Faith Demands Synergy 81

9th Principle
Stay Healthy 90

10th Principle
It's A Matter of Time 100

11th Principle
It's Never Too Late 110

1st Principle

Give God the Glory!

According to Ephesians 1:12, we are created by God that we; who first trusted in Christ, should be to the praise of His glory. Give God praise – which gives Him glory!

Ephesians 1:5-6

"Having predestinated us into the adoption of children by Jesus Christ to Himself, according to the good pleasure of His will, to the praise of the glory of His grace, wherein He hath made us accepted in the beloved"

Glorification

As Christians we believe that we are empowered by God through the Christ that has all things under His feet. In other words, Christ has conquered the world, therefore, through him we can also be conquerors.

First of all; we glorify God by surrendering to His sovereignty. We do this by not putting physical or material considerations above transcendent principles; such as love, caring and self-sacrifice. We live today in a time when many people are preoccupied with the physical appearance of things, rather than the essence of the thing, or what ultimate meaning the thing truly gives to their lives. However, what we can never forget is that all physical beauty fades, which means that it alone can never be the sole determiner for our actions, or our behaviors.

Numbers 4:15

"And when Aaron and his sons have finished covering the sanctuary and all the furnishings of the sanctuary, when the camp is set to go, then the sons of Kohath shall come to carry them; but they shall not touch any holy thing, lest they die."

God wanted the Ark carried by servants, not men chosen by kings.

The lesson for us involves the problem inherent in being 'status conscious'. Status has nothing to do with human worth. I'm not saying that status is bad in and of itself. I'm saying that status can never be allowed to define your humanity, or the worth of any person.

Status arises out of the human instinctual need for order, rather than serving as a means by which men de-value others, or others de-value themselves. Status arises out of man's inability to understand innately how he or she fits into the human jigsaw puzzle that is our human existence. It is because of this weakness that status comes into existence. However, in many instances rather than the source for human freedom and the actualization of individual purpose, status becomes a deterrent especially in the hands of tyrannical men or women.

Status, in many societies and communities, has come to denote human worth. For example, how much money you have in your bank account, the kind of clothes that you are able to afford, or simply the way that you dress, the car you drive, the schools that you attend, even the church that you attend; all of these things have come to represent human value.

Glorification is possible because He has put all things under Christ feet.

1. We glorify God by surrendering to His sovereignty.

We do this by not putting physical, or material considerations above spiritual principles. We live in a world that glorifies appearances. For example, Americans waste $276 billion dollars every year on drinking, smoking, and taking illegal drugs, just to feed their obsession with the material world.

God wanted the Ark carried by servants, not men chosen by kings. David chose 30 thousand of his best men, however, God reserves the right to choose the least of us to carry his glory.

Numbers 4:15
"And when Aaron and his sons have finished covering the sanctuary and all the furnishings of the sanctuary, when the camp is set to go, then the sons of Kohath shall come to carry them; but they shall not touch any holy thing, lest they die.

Today, we live in a time when mankind seeks to make the transcendent things of God conform to their cultural, social, or political point of view. To touch the sacred things of God is to allow our prejudices, our fears, our limited contextual views about the world, or the people in the world, to alter and confuse God's ultimate intent for the world, and its people.

God choses servants, because servants have no will or purpose of their own. They are completely surrendered to the purposes and the will of God. God's purpose and will for us must always be seen through the prism of our sacrifice, never through the window of our desires.

Sacrifice then, is the principle around which all obedience to God must revolve. Whether it is the sacrifice of our pride, our egoism, our cultural or social selves, or our material possessions, we are called always to sacrifice, never to domination.

2. When we start owning the things of God, God ceases to be sovereign.

2 Samuel 6:5-8

Then David and all the house of Israel played music ***before the LORD on all kinds of*** instruments of ***Fir wood, on harps, on stringed instruments, on tambourines, on sistrums, and on cymbals.***

And when they came to Nachon's threshing floor, Uzzah put out his hand ***to the ark of God and took hold of it, for the oxen stumbled. Then the anger of the LORD was aroused against Uzzah, and God struck him there for*** his ***error; and he died there by the ark of God. And David became angry because of the LORD's outbreak against Uzzah; and he called the name of the place Perez Uzzah to this day.***

It is David's anger that causes him to question both the judgement and sovereignty of God. David's attempt to circumvent obedience to God with celebration was not enough. Celebration alone will not keep you away from the threshing floor. The threshing floor is a place where the wheat is separated from the chaff. Spiritually it is those places where God removes those things which are bad for us from us.

Celebration without obedience leads to annihilation or complete destruction. According to the story the oxen got stuck in the mud, Uzzah who was caught in the wrong place at the wrong time died because he was an accidental participant in David's act of disobedience. The Ark should have been carried on the shoulders of the Levites, rather than on a cart.

1 Chronicles 15:15
And the children of the Levites bare the ark of God upon their shoulders with the staves thereon, as Moses commanded according to the word of the LORD.

The lesson here is that we have to be careful about who we surround ourselves with. We can never yield to the mandates, or the directions of groups or people unless we are sure that they are in compliance with the will and purposes of God. For example; you may not be driving the car, however, if a crime is committed by someone while you are in the car, you become an accomplice to that crime.

2 Samuel 6:9

David was afraid of the Lord that day; and he said, "How can the ark of the Lord come to me?" So David would not move the ark of the Lord with him into the City of David; but David took it aside into the house of Obed-Edom the Gittite. The ark of the Lord remained in the house of Obed-Edom the Gittite three months. And the Lord blessed Obed-Edom and all his household.

David's question in Verse 9 is a very fundamental question to this text.
"How can the ark of the Lord come to me?"

This question calls us all to determine how we can live safely surrounded by the security and promise of God.
Matthew 16:24, "If anyone wishes to come after Me, he must deny himself, and take up his cross and follow Me."

True servanthood calls upon us to interrupt our comfortable place in order to accommodate the purposes and plans of God. Obed-Edom personifies this servant posture that God expects of us. He takes the ark, without fear, or reservation; even in light of the fact that, Uzzah had lost his life by simply taking hold of the ark. He allows himself and his family to be used by the king as sacrifices.

The ark stayed in his house for three months, and during that time God blessed him and his household. Being a servant opens the door for blessings for you, and for those who are a part of your household. Your children, grandchildren and all who are a part of your posterity.

> *2 Samuel 6:12-15*
>
> ***Now it was told King David, saying, "The Lord has blessed the house of ObedEdom and all that belongs to him, because of the ark of God." So David went and brought up the ark of God from the house of Obed-Edom to the City of David with gladness. And so it was, when those bearing the ark of the Lord had gone six paces, that he sacrificed oxen and fatted sheep. Then David danced before the Lord with all his might; and David was wearing a linen ephod. So David and all the house of Israel brought up the ark of the Lord with shouting and with the sound of the trumpet.***

In order to glorify God, we must be willing to endure the scorn of those close to us. What David learned is that serving God will humble you. Upon learning this lesson and being finally obedient to God, he brought the ark to the city. He then danced before the Lord, giving God self-sacrificial praise. This is praise that is unpretentious. This is what God demands. It doesn't matter what our earthly status may be, we must be willing to ignore men, in order to please God.

Like Michal in our text, men may question our behavior. They may think that what we do in appreciation for God's goodness is not necessary, but our intent must always be to please God with our absolute surrender to Him and His will. Those who laugh at us, or who mock our praise risk the penalty of baroness.

Michal, the daughter of Saul, had no children. The concept of baroness also has to do with prosperity, or blessings. We put our blessings in jeopardy when we ridicule the service, sacrifice, and praise of other people. We must always remember that God is in control.

2 Samuel 6:16-20

Now as the ark of the Lord came into the City of David, Michal, Saul's daughter, looked through a window and saw King David leaping and whirling before the Lord; and she despised him in her heart. So they brought the ark of the Lord, and set it in its place in the midst of the tabernacle that David had erected for it. Then David offered burnt offerings and peace offerings before the Lord. And when David had finished offering burnt offerings and peace offerings, he blessed the people in the name of the Lord of hosts. Then he distributed among all the people, among the whole multitude of Israel, both the women and the men, to everyone a loaf of bread, a piece of meat, and a cake of raisins. So all the people departed, everyone to his house. Then David returned to bless his household. And Michal the daughter of Saul came out to meet David, and said, "How glorious was the king of Israel today, uncovering himself today in the eyes of the maids of his servants, as one of the base fellows shamelessly uncovers himself!"

2 Samuel 6:21-23

So David said to Michal, "It was before the Lord, who chose me instead of your father and all his house, to appoint me ruler over the people of the Lord, over Israel. Therefore; I will play music before the Lord. And I will be even more undignified than this, and will be humble in my own sight. But as for the maidservants of whom you have spoken, by them I will be held in honor." Therefore, Michal the daughter of Saul had no children to the day of her death.

NOTES:

1st Principle – Give GOD the Glory!

QUESTIONS

Where does it state that we were created by God, for his glory? In your own words, please explain how we were specifically picked.

_____
_____
_____
_____
_____
_____
_____
_____
_____

What are three suggestions on how you can be obedient in your personal praise, and why?

1. _____
   _____
2. _____
   _____
3. _____
   _____

TRUE or FALSE

The "Threshing Floor" is the spiritual example where God removes from us the things that are not good.

                True   False

Have you ever experienced the 'Threshing Floor?' Please explain.

_____
_____
_____
_____
_____
_____
_____

Explain why "Celebration" does not circumvent "Obedience".

_____
_____
_____
_____
_____
_____

Dr. Jeffrey stated, "Sacrifice is the principle whereas all obedience to God must revolve." Explain this concept or give an example.

_____
_____
_____
_____
_____
_____

Give an example of "Self-Sacrificial Praise.

_____
_____
_____
_____
_____
_____

In your own words, please explain why David place the Ark in the house of Obed-Edom, and why did he remove it.

_____

_____

_____

_____

_____

_____

_____

_____

_____

_____

_____

2nd Principle

Keep A Positive Attitude

The story of Joseph in the bible is a story of a man who exhibited great patience. Patience can be defined as 'The ability to remain calm when dealing with a difficult or annoying situation, task, or person.' It can mean persevering in the face of delay or provocation without acting on negative annoyance or anger. Not reacting under stress or strain even when faced with long-term difficulties.

Joseph demonstrated absolute trust in the destiny that was given to him by God. Joseph was one of the twelve tribes of Israel. His father Jacob favored him and gave him a special coat of many colors.

When Joseph was 17, he had two dreams – Joseph and his brothers were gathering grains, his brothers grain bowed down to his grain. The second dream – the sun, moon and stars bowed to Joseph.

It was because of these dreams and the preferential treatment that he received by his father that Joseph's brothers became very jealous of him. One day Jacob sent Joseph to visit his brothers in Shechem, where they were tending their sheep. The brothers saw this as an opportunity take their resentment out on Joseph, so they took him and threw him into a pit. Joseph, because of his brothers, begins his adult life in a pit.

This story points us to the fact that in this life, you don't have to be at fault to be thrown into the pit. There are many people who are forced by the circumstances of birth, to begin their lives in a pit. These are people who may have been born into poverty, or into war torn countries. These are people who may have been born with a propensity for drug addiction, or some other form of genetic disorder, that would handicap their lives, and cause them to begin life without, or on an uneven playing field. It is these kinds of circumstances that led many to see themselves as less than, or hopeless victims of a "pit" reality.

The primary lesson of the story of Joseph is that you don't have to be at fault to be thrown into a pit. For example, I was born the second son in a family of sixteen children, fourteen boys and two girls. I was born into a pit of poverty, and to some extent neglect. We were very poor; therefore, my mother had to work as well as my father just to provide enough money so that we could live.

However, my pit was not as deep as some others who were born into much more dire circumstance. For example, Oprah Gail Winfrey was born to unmarried parents who were separated soon after she was born. During her early childhood she was raised by her grandmother on a farm. Occasionally, Oprah lived with her mother in a Milwaukee ghetto, which was an extremely poor and dangerous neighborhood.

It was during this period of her life that she was sexually abused starting at the age of nine years old. Today Oprah is one of the wealthiest women in America. Your potential does not have to be determined by your pit.

Another example of a person who transcended the pit was Harriet Tubman. Harriet Tubman, an African American slave, escaped to freedom in the North in 1849 to become the most famous conductor on the Underground Railroad. Tubman risked her life to lead hundreds of family members and other slaves from the plantation system to freedom.

The fundamental thing that we must all do when we discover ourselves in a pit is to continue to believe in our promised destiny. In order to do that we can't spend our time attributing blame either on ourselves, or to others.

The purpose of the pit, whether it is the one that Joseph's brothers put him in or the jail that Potiphar later had him thrown into, was to create within him a consciousness of blame. It is this consciousness that traps us in the pits of this life. Pits by their very nature are designed to kill our dreams, destroy our initiative, and just simply make us give up on life itself. The bible teaches us in Revelations 3:8, that God has given us all an open door.

Revelations 3:8

I know thy works: behold, I have set before thee an open door, and no man can shut it: for thou hast a little strength, and hast kept my word, and hast not denied my name.

In addition, **Romans 8:28** teaches us that *"All things work together for good to those who love God, to those who are called according to His purpose."*

Pits serve to separate us from the material phenomena that is in our way. There are many things that we have that are in the way of our destiny. Sometimes along with great loss comes greater discovery. Oprah Winfrey put it this way, *"Challenges are gifts that force us to search for a new center of gravity. Don't fight them. Just find a new way to stand."*

In addition, I believe that pits force us into God' journey for our lives, for in the end the worth of our lives are not defined by our journey, but they are defined by where that journey takes us. Therefore, we can never be victorious when we come out of the pit with a pit consciousness. Jesus told Lazarus to take off those grave clothes. Just because you went through the 'grave' doesn't mean that the 'grave' was your destination. Jay Z, the rapper once wrote, "Change clothes and go!" There is no such thing as ghettofabulous … the pit was never your home.

The primary indication that we are stuck in a pit consciousness is the inability to forgive. God wants your deliverance to serve as the impetus for the eventual deliverance of your brothers and sisters, Joseph's family was saved because of his willingness to forgive.

In the Joseph story, Joseph was sold to Ishmaelite traders, these traders took Joseph to Egypt. Egypt in the story represents the place where God's predetermined destiny for Joseph was intended to take place. Pits then serve a purpose that position us into areas where we can act out the purposes of God in our lives.

After coming to Egypt, Joseph was purchased by Potiphar who was an Egyptian officer and head of Pharaoh's kitchen. However, while working in Potiphar's house, Joseph was nudged even closer to his destiny by suffering additional hardship. Potiphar's wife accused him of improper advances towards her and her husband, not believing Joseph, had him thrown into prison which can be considered just another pitfall.

However, just as the first pit was responsible for him coming to Egypt, the second pit put him miraculously into the court of Pharaoh. While in prison Joseph became well-liked by the chief jailor who put him in charge of all the other prisoners including Pharaoh's butler and baker. One night both the butler and the baker had strange dreams. Joseph interpreted the dreams of both men. According to Joseph's interpretation, the baker was to die in three days while the butler would be restored to his position. Everything happened just as Joseph had predicted. The baker died, and the butler was restored.

The butler promised Joseph that he would help facilitate his release, however he forgot his promise and Joseph languished in prison for two more years before the butler would remember him. Finally, the king was told the events that happened in prison and Joseph was summoned to interpret Pharaoh's dream, predicting a famine that was going to cover Egypt and all the surrounding areas.

Joseph successfully interpreted Pharaoh's dream and out of appreciation, Pharaoh made him the second most powerful man in Egypt. Thus, setting the stage for Joseph to become the means by which his family survived the famine.

There are three things that we should always value as it relates to the story of Joseph:

1. **Never give up on your dreams even when it seems that everything is going against you.** There is always more than one way to arrive at your destination, and many times that path goes through the pits of this life.

2. **Don't allow yourself to become bitter and cynical.** These twin towers will soon overwhelm your consciousness, and change both your attitude, and behavior. This change in perspective is all that is needed to cause us to give in to the call to selfindulgence, a call personified in the text by Potiphar's wife's attempt to seduce Joseph.

3. **Forgiveness is always an essential part of fulfilling our destiny**. God's ultimate purpose for us is to use the pits that men throw us into as the means for us to be the instrument for the redemption of the men who threw us into the pits. We must always take seriously the words of Jesus Christ from the cross, **"Father forgive them for they know not what they do."**

The song writer put it this way; *"I've had many tears and sorrows, questions about tomorrow, there have been times when I didn't know right from wrong. But in every situation, God gave consolation that my trials had come to make me strong. Through it all, I learned to trust in Jesus, I've learned to trust in God. Through it all, I've learned to depend on God's word."*

NOTES:

_____

_____

_____

_____

_____

_____

_____

_____

_____

_____

_____

2nd Principle – Keep A Positive Attitude

QUESTIONS

Can you give any example where the "Pit" became a blessing?

_____
_____
_____
_____
_____

What is an indication that we are stuck in a Pit-consciousness?

_____
_____
_____
_____
_____

Where in the bible can you find the story of Joseph and his eleven brothers? Can you name the twelve tribes of Israel?

_____
_____
_____
_____
_____

How did Joseph's dilemma work for God's purpose and for the good of the Israelite?

_____

_____

_____

_____

_____

_____

What works for the good of those who love the Lord? How is that?

_____

_____

_____

_____

_____

_____

Dr. Jeffrey stated that the worth of our lives is not defined by our journey but is defined by where that journey takes us. Can you explain this concept?

_____

_____

_____

_____

_____

TRUE or FALSE

When we become cynical and bitter, we can overwhelm our self-consciousness.

                True   False

God uses the pit for redemption; especially for those who put us there, in the pit.

                True   False

Romans 8:28 is a parable.

                True   False

Explain why "Forgiveness" is necessary.

_____

_____

_____

_____

Explain 'Patience' and what it means to you?

_____

_____

_____

_____

_____

_____

3rd Principle

Appreciate What You Have

Matthew 25:18

"But he that had received one went and digged in the earth, and hid his lord's money."

In the story of the Talents, the bible defines for us the natural inequities of human existence. We are all born different, with different abilities, different mental capacity, and different resources. Some people are born rich, while others are born in poverty. Some are born with the ability to learn quickly, while others struggle just to understand the simplest facts.

For example, Stephen Hawking is one of the most well-known physicists in the world, and he was able to achieve that recognition in spite of being diagnosed with ALS, or better known as Lou Gerhrigs disease when he was only 21 years of age. He could only speak with the assistance of a computer and for most of his life he was a fulltime powerchair-user. However, he never used his disability as an excuse to give up on his desire to study the universe, specifically the framework of general relativity and quantum mechanics.

Another example is Stevie Wonder. Stevie Wonder is a musician, singer and songwriter who was born blind. He was born six weeks early, and therefore the blood vessels at the back of his eyes had not yet reached the front and aborted their growth causing him to be blind from birth. Considered a child prodigy, Stevie signed with his first record label at age 11, Motown's Tamla label, and he's been performing since. Over his wildly successful music career, Stevie has recorded more than 30 U.S. top ten hits.

The fundamental question that we must all contemplate is the fairness of life itself. Why is it that some are born with a greater advantage than others, and why does God allow this kind of disparity if He is a God of love? In the story defined in Matthew 25, the message teaches us that happiness and success does not come from what we have, but it comes from what we do with what we have.

Most human dissatisfaction with life comes from the simple belief that life, or the situation or circumstance that a person might find themselves in, is unfair; or created by unfair or oppressive realities. Once we have reasoned that life is unfair, we set ourselves up to fight against life itself, rather than to concentrate on seeking a resolution, or a strategic advantage over our perceived or actual, disadvantages or suffered disparities.

> **Matthew 25:18**
> ***"But he that had received one went and digged in the earth, and hid his lord's money."***

The point being made here is that the individual who received less than the two others, one receiving five, and the other two, felt cheated. He felt like life was not being fair to him. There are two important things to point out about this verse; first, he hid what he was given, and second, what he was given was not his to hide; it was his lord's money. *He hid what he was given!*

Life according to this text contains gifts both plural and singular from God. Every life has a gift. No one born into this world is without a gift, however, some gifts are considered by us to be more consequential than others. This human judgement in many instances goes against the teachings of Christ Himself.

> **Matthew 20:16**
> ***"So the last shall be first and the first shall be last."***

This according to the bible is the ultimate justice of life.

To hide your gift, is to conceal your gift, to not display your gift, to feel that you are somehow not as good as others. He hid his gift in the earth. He buried his gift beneath common things of the world. It could be addiction, anger, resentment, prejudice, or jealousy. These are just some of the things that we hide the gifts given to us beneath.

The result of hiding one's gift is bitterness, and cynicism, which is displayed in Matthew.

> **Matthew 25:24-25**
> *Then he which had received the one talent came and said, Lord, I knew you that you are a hard man, reaping where you have not sown, and gathering where you have not strawed. And I was afraid and went and hid your talent in the earth so there you have that which is yours.*

In other words, I was preserving it for you, rather than using it to demonstrate the ultimate justice of God, by showing how God could take even one talent and turn it into an abundance. The response of God to this mindset is made emphatically clear in verse 26-27.

> **Matthew 25:26-27**
> *"His lord answered and said unto him, you wicked and slothful servant, you know that I reap where I sowed not, and gathered where I have not strawed. You should therefore ought to have put my money to the exchangers, and then at my coming I should have received mine own with usury."*

The bible also teaches us:

> **2 Corinthians 4:7,**
>
> ***"But we have this treasure in earthen vessels, that the excellency of the power may be of God and not of us."***

In many instances the expressed purposes of 'lack' is to demonstrate through our faith both the compassion, and the deliverance power of God.

The other aspect teaches us that God does promise increase to all who are willing to take what he has given them and use it to create more.

> **Matthew 25:21**
>
> ***"Well done good and faithful servant, you have been faithful over a few things, I will make you ruler over many."***

In this statement the bible underscores the principle of success, and it is simply, being faithful over the few things that we might possess. This principle defines the justice of God. Faithfulness to one's purpose as identified by their gifts, is the key to being successful. In addition, it is also the key to even a greater level of success than even your gifts could bring you.

> **Matthew 25: 28**
>
> ***"Take therefore the talent from him, and give it to him that has ten talents."***

As we read this text many would interpret this scripture to mean that all of us can be millionaires or billionaires, if we simply are faithful to a particular task. However, this is not the meaning of the text, this text is not just about money, even though it includes every form of security that we may need in this world. This text is about being faithful to the purposes, and gifts that we have been given.

We must invest these gifts in the realities of this world, and we are promised that the investment will bring about positive benefits to us. The bible teaches us in Mark 10, that all faith investments will pay off.

Mark 10:29-30

"And Jesus answered and said, verily I say unto you, there is no man that hath left house or brethren or sisters, or father, or mother, or wife, or children, or lands, for my sake and the gospel's, who will not receive an hundredfold now in this time, houses, and brethren, and sisters, and mothers, and children, and lands, with persecutions; and in the world to come eternal life.

There are at least five important take-a-ways from this text:

1. **Always appreciate what you have been given in this life**. Life trumps all situations. There are people that are born poor, disadvantaged, with a handicap, blind, in impoverished countries, in the middle of war, rich, in every conceivable situation imaginable, however, their birth should never define their possibilities. To appreciate what you have been given does not mean to be satisfied with what you have been given, but merely to see it for what it is, something to begin with. Everybody has something to begin with.

    Believe in what you have been given, without hesitation or doubt, trust God, and you will trust yourself, love God, and you will love yourself, believe in God, and you will believe in yourself. Doubt creates fear, and fear creates hesitancy, which leads to a desire to escape, which leads invariably to losing it all. Mathew 25:28 states, *"take therefore the talent from him, and give it unto him which hath ten talents."*

2. **Never be afraid to invest it all to pursue God's purpose for your life**. The bible is filled with stories of people who were willing to give up everything in order to fulfill their purpose. Whether it is Abraham in Genesis 22, who stood ready to sacrifice his only son or in the Book of Ruth, where Ruth followed her mother in law, Naomi to a strange land or in Daniel 6, where Daniel was facing a den of lions. These are all stories of men and women willing against all odds to believe in the legitimacy of what they have

been given. Like these men and women, the time will come in all our lives, when we will have to exhibit similar faith in our destiny, are God's plan for our lives.

3. **Don't be envious of others**. Another fundamental lesson of the bible is that more is not always better. We learn this lesson when we see Pharaoh's army drown, as he pursues the people of God, in Exodus 14-15. We see in again in the story of Job, a good man who loses everything, but does not give up his faith.

This is a reoccurring theme though out the bible. What other people have, can never define the destiny that God has planned for you. The true challenge is to stay focused on your destiny, because there are pit falls on every road, even those that are paved.

4. **Investments never stop, and neither does increase**. There is never a time in this life when we can be like the rich man described in Luke.

> **Luke 16:19-31**
> *"There was a rich man who was dressed in purple and fine linen and lived in luxury every day. At his gate was a beggar named Lazarus, covered with sores, and longing to eat what fell from the rich man's table. Even the dogs came and licked his sores."*

No matter where we are in life, we will never be able to escape the urgency of our purpose, and the immediacy of our responsibility. It will always be at our door, but so will the fact of possibilities for increase.

5. **Increase will come, even in the middle of persecution**. There is no human difficulty, or dilemma that can stop our increase. Trouble rather than being a deterrent to increase, in many instances it the thing that stimulates, or opens the door to increase.

This point is demonstrated in a powerful way by the final act of Jesus Christ on the earth. His passion, His suffering, rather than closing the door on the potential of his purpose, actually opened the door wider, and gave to Him power and dominion not just over some things but over all things.

NOTES

3rd Principle – Appreciate What You Have

QUESTIONS

How do you reconcile the belief by many that 'Life's simply not fair'?

_____
_____
_____
_____
_____

What are some advantages that we call God given gifts?

_____
_____
_____
_____

Why would anyone hide their God given gifts?

_____
_____
_____
_____
_____

TRUE or FALSE

When we trust God, we have more trust in ourselves.

                True   False

To appreciate what we have been given is to be satisfied with what we have.

                True   False

Everyone is born with a gift.

                True   False

Increase can come in the middle of persecution.

                True   False

More is always better.

                True   False

Explain why we can never measure our worth by the prosperity of others.

_____

_____

_____

_____

Dr Jeffrey stated that our true challenge is to stay focused on our destiny. What is your destiny and what are some of the techniques you use to stay focused?

_____

_____

_____

_____

_____

4th Principle

Stay Woke

1 Peter 5:8

"Be sober, be vigilant; because your adversary the devil, as a roaring lion, walketh about, seeking whom he may devour."

Sobriety is the key to living a productive and meaningful life. To be sober as the bible commands us, is to be serious, sensible and solemn. Being serious about our lives, involves four basic considerations.

1. **We must take every decision that affects our life seriously**. There are no unimportant decisions as it relates to how we are going to live our life. We do this by paying attention to the things that really matter. For example, things like God's purpose for our lives, our family, our children, our community, we can't allow ourselves to become side-tracked by the trivial stuff of life. This is stuff like, how we look as a woman or a man, whether we are too short, too tall, too fat, or too skinny. In the scheme of things, these things don't really matter as much as we may think that they do. Things matter only when they are essential to our very existence.

2. **God matters**! Without Him we would not have existence, or a divine purpose. Nor would we have the grace needed to both forgive ourselves and others; and be forgiven. Tillich says that, "God is the ground of our being," He is essential.

3. **Family matters ... I mean mother, father, and siblings as well as wife, and even close friends**. They matter because family is the first source for our agreement. If we are to accomplish our purpose in this life, we must have agreement, and that agreement should begin with the family.

   However, family agreement can be jeopardized by our neglect, or in the case of a wife, husband, or friends, by both neglect or being unequally yoked together in relationships that we entered without being woke.

   Children matter because they are our seed, and as seed they must be nurtured, without nurture, they will have difficulty achieving the potential that God intended for them. Lost children, or children with stunted growth are usually children that have not been nurtured or taken as seriously as God intended for them to be taken.

4. **Community also matters**. As humans we do not live in isolation. We live in neighborhoods and communities; we have a responsibility to both our neighbors and our communities.

   Matthew 5,
   "Ye are the salt of the earth, the light of the world, a city that is set on a hill that cannot be hid."

   Jesus talked about this responsibility to community and neighbor.

   Luke 10:25-37.
   And Jesus answering said, A certain man went down from Jerusalem to Jericho, and fell among thieves, which stripped him of his raiment, and wounded him, and departed, leaving him half dead. And by chance where came down a certain priest that way: and when he saw him, he passed by on the other side. And likewise a Levite, when he was at the place, came and looked on him, and passed by on the other side. But a certain Samaritan, as he journeyed, came where he was: and when he saw him, he had compassion on him, And went to him, and

bound up his wounds, pouring in oil and wine, and set him on his own beast, and brought him to an inn, and took care of him.

In this story restorative help was given to a stranger, simply because of his need. This help was given only after two religious leaders had refused to give any assistance. The text then concludes by asking the question, ***"so which of these three do you think was a neighbor to him who fell among thieves?"*** So, these are the essentials, God, family, children, and community.

To stay woke we must practice perseverance, or steadfastness and we must not allow any difficulty or problem to stop us from achieving eventual success.

Hebrews 12:18-24

"***You have not come to a mountain that can be touched and that is burning with fire; to darkness, gloom and storm; to a trumpet blast or to such a voice speaking words that those who heard it begged that no further word be spoken to them. But you have come to Mount Zion, to the city of the living God, the heavenly Jerusalem. You have come to thousands upon thousands of angels in joyful assembly to the church of the firstborn whose names are written in heaven. You have come to God, the judge of all, to the spirits of the righteous made perfect, to Jesus the mediator of a new covenant, and to the sprinkled blood that speaks a better word than the blood of Abel.***"

With this scripture in mind we must never allow our expectations to be defused by momentary setbacks.

We don't always get to define our struggles, some of them are predetermined, either by birth, or the circumstances of our lives. However, we can define how we struggle, and the outcome of that struggle.

Dietrich Bonhoeffer, a German pastor and theologian, was arrested in 1943 because of his stand against Hitler. He was tried and executed by hanging because of his stance, however before dying he wrote these words, *"we must be ready to allow ourselves to be interrupted by God....We must not assume that our schedule is our own to manage, but allow it to be arranged by God."*

In this statement and with the sacrifice of his life, Bonhoeffer redefines for us the meaning of a successful or victorious life.

We are not all called to pay the price that Bonhoeffer paid, however we are all called to be just as committed as he was to the cause of Christ. To do this we must redefine what it means to be victorious in life. Bonhoeffer states that *"cheap grace is the grace we bestow on ourselves. Cheap grace is the preaching of forgiveness without requiring repentance, baptism without church discipline, Communion without confession…Cheap grace is grace without discipleship, grace without the cross, grace without Jesus Christ, living and incarnate."* Ultimate power, and capacity for Christians comes only when we are totally committed to the purposes and mission that is given to us by God.

Our eventual victory lies in the fact that God uses human capacity to both encourage His people and to defeat His enemies. Like David, who defeated Goliath, we know that God will equip us for the task. The challenge for us is to avoid self-indulgence.

> **2 Samuel 11:2-4**
> ***It happened, late one afternoon, when David arose from his couch and was walking on the roof of the king's house, that he saw from the roof a woman bathing; and the woman was very beautiful. ³ And David sent and inquired about the woman. And one said, "Is not this Bathsheba, the daughter of Eliam, the wife of Uriah the Hittite?" ⁴ So David sent messengers and took her, and she came to him, and he lay with her.***

In Joshua 7, the bible tells us about the story of Achan.

> **Joshua 7**
>
> ***But the people of Israel broke faith in regard to the devoted things, for Achan the son of Carmi, son of Zabdi, son of Zerah, of the tribe of Judah, took some of the devoted things. And the anger of the L<small>ORD</small> burned against the people of Israel.***

During the conquest of Jericho, the Israelites were instructed to destroy everything in the city with the exception of Rahab and her family. The gold, silver, bronze, and iron were to be put into the tabernacle treasury. Achan, however, because of his self-indulgence; took some of the gold and silver for himself.

> **Joshua 7:19**
>
> ***Then Joshua said to Achan, "My son, give glory to the L<small>ORD</small> God of Israel and give praise to him. And tell me now what you have done; do not hide it from me."***

Achan confesses to have taken a robe, two hundred shekels of silver and a fifty-shekel bar of gold. Because of Achan's sin, Israel was defeated by their enemies when they sought to conquer the next city of Ai.

The story illustrates the fact that God is intolerant of self-indulgence. It also teaches us that our self-indulgence not only affects us, but others as well. In the case of Achan, he put the promises of God for Israel in jeopardy. Therefore, the story reveals to us that our power and capacity is directly related to whether or not we can control our selfish inclinations.

We must always put the needs of the Kingdom before our own needs. We must be true to our covenant relationship with God. It is a spiritual relationship that produces physical manifestations.

A true sign of power is being able to shake off the temptation that Satan seeks to use to bind us. Today we are given the power and the authority to enter into an abundant life.

We know that we have authentic victory when we can say as Paul said in Philippians.

> **Philippians 4:11-14**
>
> *"Not that I speak in respect of want; for I have learned in whatsoever state I am, therewith to be content. I know both how to be abased, and I know how to abound; everywhere and in all things, I am instructed both to be full and to be hungry both to abound and to suffer need. I can do all things through Christ who give me strength."*

Finally, it is believed that Thomas Edison failed approximately 1000, times before creating the light bulb. Some believe that it was close to 10,000 times. He famously was quoted as saying *"I have not failed I've just found 10,000 ways that won't work."* There are three important things that we always remember in order to stay woke:

1. **We must understand that hard work is the key to achieving the promises of God.** We can never be afraid of working hard for as long as it takes, without regard for the many times that we won't succeed.

2. **We must always remain faithful to the vision or purpose of our hard work.** The bible teaches us in **Isaiah 40:31, *"They that wait on the Lord shall renew their strength, they shall mount up on wings like as eagles, they shall run and not be weary, and they shall walk, and not faint."***

3. **Our lives, and the things that we are seeking to do in our lives must always be open to be directed or redirected by the move of God. Proverbs 3:5-6**, states that we should *"trust in the Lord with all our hearts and lean not to our own understanding. In all our ways acknowledge Him and He shall direct our paths."*

NOTES:

_____
_____
_____
_____
_____
_____
_____
_____
_____
_____

Something to Ponder

Hebrews 12:

You have not come to a mountain that can't be touched … But you have come to Mount Zion, to the city of the living God ... You have come to thousands upon thousands of angels in joyful assembly to the church of the firstborn whose names are written in heaven. You have come to God!!

4TH Principle – STAY WOKE!

QUESTIONS

Explain the four basic considerations when we are serious about life.

1. _____
   _____

2. _____
   _____

3. _____
   _____

4. _____
   _____

How can self-indulgence keep us from being focused?

_____
_____
_____
_____
_____

Give an example of "Cheap Grace" as describe by Bonhoeffer?

_____
_____
_____
_____
_____
_____
_____

TRUE or FALSE

Things only matter when they are essential to our existence.

                True   False

Once we have our plan for success, we must never be open for redirection.

                True   False

Ultimate power comes when we are totally committed to God's purpose for our life.

                True   False

We can never define how we struggle.

                True   False

Commitments are spiritual that can lead to physical manifestations.

                True   False

Give an example where God equipped you for a specific task.

___

Explain "Authentic Victory" as described in Principle 4.

___

To be "Woke" we must practice perseverance. Why is that important?

___

5th Principle

The Power of Investment

Ecclesiastes 11:1

"Cast thy bread upon the waters; for thou shalt find it after many days."

All prosperity both economic and spiritual began with investments. An investment is defined as devoting of resources, giving of time, talent, money, emotional energy for a purpose, or to achieve something in return. Investments are always given with the idea that there will be a return.

Mark 10:29

"Truly I tell you, no one who has left home or brothers or sister or mother or father for me and the gospel will fail to receive a hundred times in this present age."

God never asks us to take risks without a guaranteed return; whether it's with our family, with our property, or through persecution. The call of God to us is that we don't value the possessions that we have today more than the multiplied wealth God wants to give us tomorrow. To understand this principle better, look at **Job 42:10**

Job 42:10

And the L<small>ORD</small> restored the fortunes of Job, when he had prayed for his friends. And the L<small>ORD</small> gave Job twice as much as he had before.

In 1 Kings, the bible tells the story of a woman who only had enough food for one more meal for both she and her son. However, God sends Elijah to her house in order to find food, because the brook where he'd been living beside had dried up. This story gives us a clear picture of how biblical investments work.

1 King 17:8-16

And the word of the LORD came unto him, saying, Arise, get thee to Zarephath, which belongeth to Zidon, and dwell there: behold, I have commanded a widow woman there to sustain thee. So he arose and went to Zarephath. And when he came to the gate of the city, behold, the widow woman was there gathering of sticks: and he called to her, and said, Fetch me, I pray thee, a little water in a vessel, that I may drink. And as she was going to fetch it, he called to her, and said, Bring me, I pray thee, a morsel of bread in thine hand. And she said, As the LORD thy God liveth, I have not a cake, but an handful of meal in a barrel, and a little oil in a cruse: and, behold, I am gathering two sticks, that I may go in and dress it for me and my son, that we may eat it, and die. And Elijah said unto her, Fear not; go and do as thou hast said: but make me thereof a little cake first, and bring it unto me, and after make for thee and for thy son. For thus saith the LORD God of Israel, The barrel of meal shall not waste, neither shall the cruse of oil fail, until the day that the LORD sendeth rain upon the earth. And she went and did according to the saying of Elijah: and she, and he, and her house, did eat many days. And the barrel of meal wasted not, neither did the cruse of oil fail, according to the word of the LORD, which he spake by Elijah.

Elijah represents the opportunity for investment that God sets before everyone who is seeking to walk in His will. These opportunities for investment are never contingent on our present capacity, but rather on God's promise for our future. Therefore, we can never response to challenges based on our capacity to perform the challenge.

She bakes the meal not because she has enough, but she bakes the meal solely because of the promise that God gives her.

> **1 Kings 17:13**
>
> *And Elijah said unto her, Fear not; go and do as thou hast said: but make me thereof a little cake first, and bring it unto me, and after make for thee and for thy son.*

Elijah tells her about the promise of God for her and her son. He states, *"Do not be afraid, go and do as you have said, but first make me a small cake of bread from what you have, and bring it to me. Afterwards, make some for yourself and your son, for this is what the Lord God of Israel says, the jar of flour will not be exhausted and the jug of oil run dry until the day the Lord sends rain on the face of the earth"*. In other words, God sends opportunities for investment not to deplete your resources in times of need but to sustain you through those times of need.

This story also represents the power of obedience, because when we act in obedience, we create security or blessings for our children. For example, it was because of Abraham's obedience that God promised to bless his seed.

> **Genesis 12:1-3**
>
> *"Now the Lord had said unto Abram, get thee out of your country, and from your kindred, and from your father's house, unto a land that I will show you, and I will make of you a great nation, and I will bless you, and make your name great; and you shall be a blessing. And I will bless them that bless you and curse them that curse you, and in you shall all families of the earth be blessed."*

In addition, it was also this woman's obedience that saved her son.

> **1 Kings 17:17** *and it came to pass that the son of the woman the mistress of the house, fell sick; and his sickness was so sore that he had no breath left in him.*

In verse 22 this story concludes with the woman's son being healed, as a result of the intervention of Elijah.

1 Kings 17:22

"and the Lord heard the voice of Elijah; and the soul of the child came into him again, and he was revived."

A truly obedient man or woman is going to always be a blessing to their family. If Elijah had not been obedient, he could not have created the situation necessary for the widow woman to have increase in the middle of a famine. Also, if she had not been obedient, her son would have never recovered from the spiral of death that sought to destroy his life.

Obedience is also necessary if we desire to ever have abundance. Jesus tell Simone Peter to launch his boat out into deep water in order to catch an abundance of fish.

Luke 5:4

Now when he had left speaking, he said unto Simon, Launch out into the deep, and let down your nets for a draught.

As a result of Peter's obedience, he caught so much fish that his net broke. Many will never experience abundance in the kingdom of God, simply because they won't allow themselves to be obedient to God's command to invest. The only power that man has is to sow. Only God has the power to grow what man has sown.

Luke 5:7

And they beckoned unto their partners, which were in the other ship, that they should come and help them. And they came, and filled both the ships, so that they began to sink.

Obedience also enables us to benefit others. The disciples caught so much fish until they had to call other fisherman over to take some of the fish in order to keep their boats from sinking. The goal of obedience is to put us into position to change the situation of others because of our abundant blessings.

We cast our bread upon the waters:

1. People who are preoccupied with negative possibilities become immobilized. We can't allow ourselves to become paralyzed by the possibility of difficulty, or the inevitability of cosmic or environmental trouble.

2. We cast our bread upon the waters because we realize as Paul states we can plant, and we can water, but it is God who gives the increase.

   1 Corinthians 3:6

   I have planted, Apollos watered; but God gave the increase.

In Matthew 7, Jesus is telling us a story about two men, one of them was wise, and one of them was foolish. In this world there are two primary ways to build success, or wealth, or abundance. One is to do it totally reliant on self, and self-serving methods. Many have been very successful living their lives this way however Jesus compares this method of achievement as building your house on the sand.

Matthew 7:24-27

Therefore whosoever heareth these sayings of mine, and doeth them, I will liken him unto a wise man, which built his house upon a rock: And the rain descended, and the floods came, and the winds blew, and beat upon that house; and it fell not: for it was founded upon a rock. And every one that heareth these sayings of mine, and doeth them not, shall be likened unto a foolish man, which built his house upon the sand: And the rain descended, and the floods came, and the winds blew, and beat upon that house; and it fell: and great was the fall of it.

The fundamental problem with this method is that sand shifts, and is totally influenced by the cosmic, or environmental realities, such as storms or individual faults and frailties. On the other hand, adopting the mindset of Christ, protects us from the changing realities of this world, and puts our destiny squarely in the hands of God.

What the bible is teaching us is that people who are preoccupied with negative possibilities become immobilized by either the possibility of the shifting sands; or the actual event of shifting sand. The story says that the house built on the sand, is eventually destroyed, while the house built on the rock, or the principles that Jesus is teaching, stands.

It is being immobilized, that prevents us from being obedient. For example, Christian we are called to be light in this world, but in-spite of this country proposing to be a Christian nation, there are 43.1 million people still living in poverty. In addition, according to the U.S. Department of Housing and Urban Development, there are 554,000, homeless people on the streets of our country.

The challenge for those of us who believe in the teachings of Jesus Christ are clear, we must cast our bread upon the waters, with the assurance that it will not return to us void, or without results. We know that we are immobilized, when we are incapable of being moved into action in the face of any present dilemma. For example, there are also presently 16.5 million refugees in the world. These are people who need to know that somebody cares about them.

According to the bible, our ultimate purpose is to manifest light.

> **1 John 7**
>
> *But if we walk in the light, as he is in the light, we have fellowship one with another,*

Light has three primary properties.

1. **It travels at the absolute upper speed limit of anything in the universe**. There is nothing faster than light. It travels at a speed of 300,000 kilometers per second, or 186,411.36 miles per second. Light travels fast, and as light we too must always be present in situations of darkness and despair. We know that the light of God will surround us and enable us as we move in His will.

2. **Light reflects**. It is reflection that allows others to see what they cannot see without our covering situations of need. That's why Jesus tells us that the *"blind can't lead the blind"*.

Matthew 5:16

Let your light so shine before men, that they may see your good works, and glorify your Father which is in heaven.

Others can see the needs, or the just cause, or the problem that needs to be solved, only if we reflect it by getting involved.

3. **Light also contains all colors, all elements of any reality**. There is no aspect of any situation that light won't reveal to us, and to others. According to scripture we are called to be the light.

The absence of light can be defined as darkness, and darkness gives birth to all that is against humanity and their need for authentic abundance. It is darkness that gives birth to poverty, despair, hopelessness, frustration, depression, and addiction, in our world.

Inherent in darkness is fear of the absence of possibilities. It is this fear that denies many, who otherwise claim to trust God; the full use of the potential He gives them for His glory and their good. These are people who never step out on God's word, who never practice the faith that they talk about. These are bench warmers, who are afraid to enter the arena, they waste their gifts, and are willing to trust God to be poor, but not trust Him to be anything else. Their attitude is to share poverty, not abundance.

Becoming light is the thing that helps us to escape the bad things that keep us in bondage. Darkness or the absence of faith keeps us imprisoned in the past of limited possibility. Faith is the switch, that turns on the light that directs us into a new future, a future that is not defined by guilt, or crippling circumstances, or persons who only desire is to keep us chained. The song writer puts it this way, *"walk in the light, the beautiful light"*.

It is this light that reveals for men and women of faith the stepping-stones that will enable us to climb higher and enable us to ultimately be what God intends for us to be. We walk in the light, not just in order to go up, but to come out of darkness.

Walking in the light is not just about our going home to be with God, but it is also about our being able to come out of the things that the enemy seeks to entrap us with down here on earth, things such as poverty, addiction, or anything that serves to oppress the human spirit.

For example, prior to his encounter with Jesus, Paul was a persecutor of the church. He would bring Christians to trials in chains at the orders of the religious authorities in Jerusalem. However, after his conversion he became the chief propagator of the faith. Instead of locking up Christians, he sought to set them free.

This is what happen to all of us who are changed. Our faith compels us to use the same energy that we used to think negatively, to think about the limitless possibilities that God has for each of us.

NOTES:

5ᵀᴴ Principle – The Power of Investments QUESTIONS

List at least three types of Investments that you have made in life.

1. _____
   _____

2. _____
   _____

3. _____
   _____

What are the benefits of these investments? How did God support your needs?

1. _____
   _____
   _____
   _____

2. _____
   _____
   _____
   _____

3. _____
   _____
   _____
   _____

Can you describe a time when God sustained you during hard times?

___

Scenario

Stephen is a retired police officer. A few years ago, his wife became a victim of a hit and run car accident. These are trying times to say the least. With the cost of her care and piling hospital charges, he mortgaged his home for the third time.

They have two beautiful daughters that he planned on sending to college. Stephen has always been a strict disciplinarian, no excuses period. If you work hard, treat people right, don't break the law, pay your bills on time, save your money, then you should be just fine.

However, Stephen wasn't fine, he was angry and disappointed that he worked hard his entire life, and will have nothing to show, nothing to leave as a legacy for his girls. How was he going to pay for college? How would you encourage Stephen?

___

TRUE or FALSE

God never asks us to take risks.

                True   False

In many ways, remembering the 'darkness' can motivate us constructively.

                True   False

Jesus is the presence of Light.

                True   False

Limited faith is always good.

                True   False

Being too preoccupied with difficulty can cause us to become immobilized.

                True   False

Obedience to God creates security for our entire family.

                True   False

Explain the three properties of light.

1. _____

_____

2. _____

_____

3. _____

_____

In your own words, can you explain Ecclesiastes 11:4

_____

_____

_____

_____

_____

_____

_____

_____

_____

Match the statements

A. Obedience

B. If we walk in the Light

C. Our purpose

D. Absence of Light

E. Cast our Bread

F. He that regards the winds

G. Waters

H. It's all vanity

I. Faith

J. I have planted, Apollo watered

____ Challenges

____ Enables us to benefit others

____ On the waters

____ God gave the increase

____ Our divinity

____ Poverty, frustration, addictions

____ Directs us to a new future

____ We have fellowship

____ To manifest Light

____ Shall not sow

Something to Ponder

As Christians, how can our investments in this life assure our reward?

6th Principle

Accepting Leadership Responsibility

Isaiah 21:11

The burden of Duman. He calleth to me out of Seir, Watchman, what of the night? Watchman, what of the night?

The New Testament defines Watchman as the Good Shepherd. Christ in the New Testament is the Good Shepherd, but as servants of Christ we are also called to be leaders of men as we follow Christ. In other words, as we follow the Good Shepherd, we ourselves are required to be shepherds or watchman. To be a good watchman is to be a good responsible leader.

The ultimate purpose of the Good Shepherd is to save the sheep, lead them to the door, where they can find pasture; sustenance, food, safety, and comfort. He keeps passage from the door, he keeps others from coming in and taking what rightfully belongs to those in his charge.

There are two basic realities that the watchman or shepherd must watch out for as it relates to protecting his sheep.

1. **The first is bad choices**. There are always other doors that do not lead to green pastures, but doors that lead to personal or collective destruction. For example, in Genesis 13, Lot decides to leave Abraham, as Abraham is following the command of God. Lot takes a group of people in an entirely different direction, only to end up as a prisoner. During his stay in Sodom, an alliance of Kings swept into Sodom. The king

of Gomorrah, the king of Admah, the king of Zebalim, and the king of Bela, were all defeated and fled to the hills. When the victors came, they took the spoils of war and took Lot and all his possessions with them.

2. **The second is to separate from your original purpose.** Lot represents an example of bad leadership that calls people to separate from the original intentions and purposes of their human responsibilities. By separating from Abraham, Lot charts a course both against the direct will of God, and a course directed by his own lustful desires.

These are the twin demons that will destroy all leaders. We must avoid them at all cost. We must always stay in the commands of God, and we can never do things simply because they are enticing or will benefit us.

What Lot demonstrates by his decision to separate from Abraham is that at any given moment everybody is a potential leader. This is one of the great challenges of leadership. However, Abraham teaches us how we should respond, there are two primary things that stand out in Abraham's response…first he allows Lot to choose what he wants, he doesn't argue with him, and second, he goes in to rescue Lot when he gets into trouble.

Authentic leadership means believing that whatever God has for you is for you. We don't have to argue or fight others who want to leave or even take from us things that we have. The only thing that can stop us from receiving the promise of God is our own faithlessness.

In addition to staying true to the commands of God, a good leader must understand what Paul talked about in Ephesians 6:10; that the enemy is constantly seeking to harm the people and the things of God. We fight the enemy by putting on the whole armor of God.

Ephesians 6:10

Finally, be strong in the Lord and in his mighty power.

II Corinthians 10:4

"for the weapons of our warfare are not carnal, but mighty through God to the pulling down of strong holds."

Today the church, although in the middle of Babylon, serves as the watchman for the things of God. In the text Duman, represents the roots from which the captives sprang. Duman is a town in Judah, it represents Godly roots. It represents the fact that we can't run away from our roots. *Roots serve a variety of functions for the tree. They absorb and transfer moisture and minerals as well as provide support for the above ground portion of the tree. When the roots of a tree dies, the tree itself will die.* This is a message for us today as we struggle with a changing world, it is a message that reminds us that we can't run away from our roots.

This was Daniel's concern in Daniel 6, in this story Daniel was faced with a leadership dilemma. The Babylon Empire had obtained dominance over Judah. As a teenager Daniel was deported to Babylon around 587 B.C. Judah fell because of its disobedience to God, and Daniel was determined not to make the same mistake.

This narrative completely engulfs the book of Daniel. On the one hand you have the people of God while on the other you have the false Gods of human invention. These are ultimately the choices that we have today, we can choose to bow down to the dictates of man or to stand up for what we know to be the will of God.

In this story prayer becomes the situation that serves as the supreme test for Daniel. However, today, there are many things that we are required to stand our ground for and against. For example, Dr. Martin Luther King died seeking to create a world without prejudice and hatred. He stated, *"injustice anywhere is a threat to justice everywhere"*. We are caught in an inescapable network of mutuality, tied in a single garment of destiny. Whatever affects one directly, affects all indirectly. He advocated for those who could not speak for themselves.

Today there is a tremendous need for men and women to do the same, whether it is the immigrants fleeing death, violence and poverty in Guatemala, or El Salvador, or hungry children in inner-city America, we like Daniel must take a stand. Dr. King also stated, *"The contemporary tendency in our society is to base our distribution on scarcity, which has vanished, and to compress our abundance into the overfed mouths of the middle and upper classes until they gag with superfluity. If democracy is to have breadth of meaning, it is necessary to adjust this inequity. It is not only moral, but it is also intelligent. We are wasting and degrading human life by clinging to archaic thinking."*

There is no effective ministry without **Shamar**, which means to **keep guard, observe, to have charge of, careful to keep, care defending**. Shamar is necessary for leadership.

Leadership at its best according to Shamar, requires intercession. Intercession can be defined as the act of intervening on behalf of another. Good leaders are always looking for ways to help others be the best that they can be. The primary principle of the life and work of Jesus Christ is that we are benefited when we intercede for others.

An example of intercession is discussed in John 5:1-15.

John 5:1-15

Sometime later, Jesus went up to Jerusalem for one of the Jewish festivals. Now there is in Jerusalem near the Sheep Gate a pool, which in Aramaic is called Bethesda and which is surrounded by five covered colonnades. Here a great number of disabled people used to lie—the blind, the lame, the paralyzed. One who was there had been an invalid for thirty-eight years. When Jesus saw him lying there and learned that he had been in this condition for a long time, he asked him, "Do you want to get well?" "Sir," the invalid replied, "I have no one to help me into the pool when the water is stirred. While I am trying to get in, someone else goes down ahead of me." Then Jesus said to him, "Get up! Pick up your mat and walk." At once the man was cured; he picked up his mat and walked. The day on which this took place was a Sabbath, and so the Jewish leaders said to the man who had been healed, "It is the Sabbath; the law forbids you to carry your mat." But he replied, "The man who made me well said to me, 'Pick up your mat and walk.'" So they asked him, "Who is this fellow who told you to pick it up and walk?" The man who was healed had no idea who it was, for

Jesus had slipped away into the crowd that was there. Later Jesus found him at the temple and said to him, "See, you are well again. Stop sinning or something worse may happen to you." The man went away and told the Jewish leaders that it was Jesus who had made him well.

In this story a man had been waiting to be healed for thirty-eight years. The question that Jesus asked him is the fundamental question that must be answered, before authentic intercession can take place. In verse 6, when Jesus asked him, do you want to be made whole … the man responds by blaming others for not helping him into the pool, so that he could get well.

Jesus teaches us in His response that intercession does not accept the excuses of those who want to blame others for their dilemma, or who want to use the intercessor as a crutch. True intercession reminds people of their God given capacity to overcome their situation. Jesus commands him to "take up his mat and walk." Christ demonstrates through this command that the responsibility of the intercessor is to create an environment for self-empowerment.

Not only does Shamar require intercession, it also requires Prophetic Discernment. The bible state in **Proverbs 29:18**, "*where there is no vision the people perish*". Vision is an essential part of being a leader. Jesus states that the "blind can't lead the blind". To lead we must not only be able to interpret God's will for right now, but we must also be able to interpret God's will for the future.

Many of the problems that we encounter in this life is because we are not walking in prophetic discernment. To walk in prophetic discernment is to be able to see things not as they are but as God intended for them to be, and to also be able to be prepared for how things are, and ready to create change when the situation demands change. For example, prophetic discernment calls upon us to be modern day Noah's. We have to be able to understand the times and call people's attention to their responsibility to God.

In addition, we must build arks that will withstand the consequences of man's continued disobedience. Without this kind of leadership many will find themselves unable to survive now or in the future.

Finally, to have true leadership, there must be a knowledge of the word of God. Leaders must stand ready to speak the word to those who may not know what God is saying in these times. However, in order to speak the word, we must know the word. We must have and understanding of the word ourselves. The bible teaches us that the people can't hear without a preacher, and that same thing goes for a teacher.

NOTES:

_____
_____
_____
_____
_____
_____
_____
_____
_____
_____
_____

6th Principle – Accepting Leadership Responsibility QUESTIONS

Watchman ... What of the night? What does this phrase mean to you?

_____

_____

_____

_____

_____

What are the two realities a Watchman must be careful of when caring for others?

1. _____

   _____

2. _____

   _____

Explain the significant of the "Whole Armor of God"?

_____

_____

_____

_____

_____

_____

Dr. Jeffrey states that authentic leadership means believing that whatever God has for you is for you. Can you share an example of "Authentic Leadership"?

_____

_____

_____

_____

_____

_____

_____

There is no intercession without Shamar. Please give an example of this component and how does it affect ones' leadership?

_____

_____

_____

_____

As defined in this text, what is "True Intercession"? Please give an example.

_____

_____

_____

Defined in this text, explain "Prophetic Discernment?"

_____

_____

_____

TRUE or FALSE

As Christians, we become Watchmen and Shepherds

                      True   False

There is no effective ministry without Shamar.

                      True   False

Whatever affects one directly affects all indirectly.

                      True   False

Prophetic Discernments calls for us to focus on the past.

                      True   False

Match the Phrase

A   The Watchman   ____ Town in Judah

B   Shamar   ____ comes to steal, kill, destroy

C   I lay down my Life   ____ Keep Guard

D   The Thief   ____ See as God intended

E   Duman   ____ On behalf of others

F   Intercession   ____ for my sheep

G   Prophetic Discernment   ____ Christ

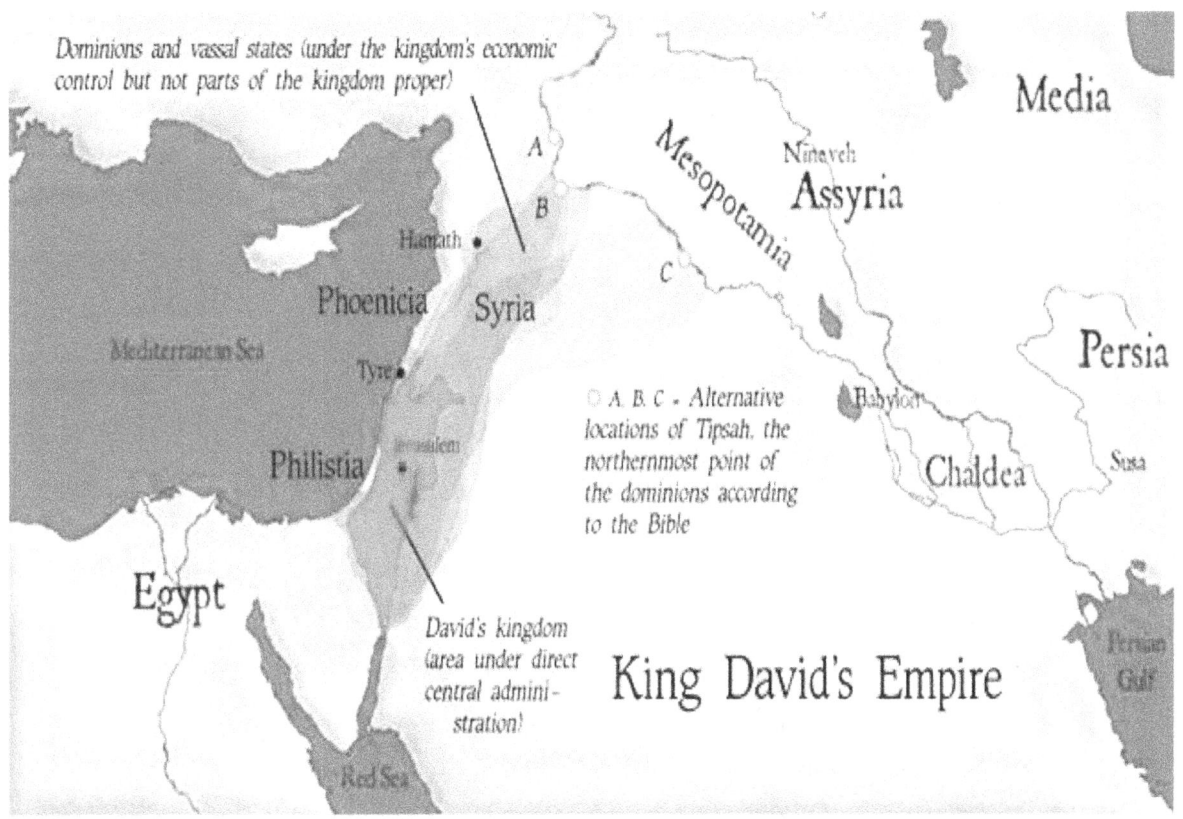

- Can you map the route King David took to deliver the Ark to Obed-Edom?
- Where did Moses cross the Red Sea?

PATH OF THE ANCIENT HEBREWS

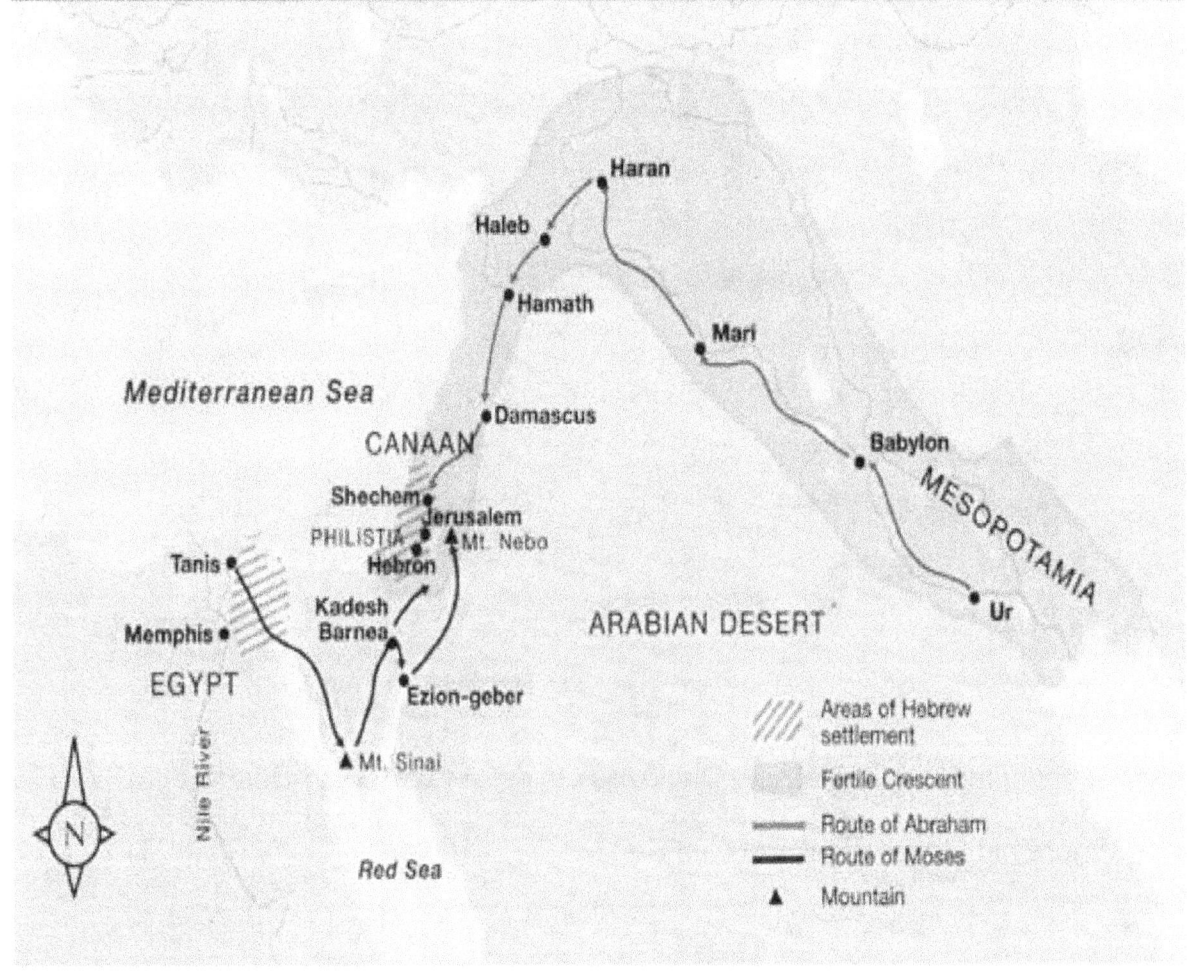

7th Principle

Use Failure as A Stepping-Stone

Failure can be the "Gateway" to success. It's okay to fail.

John 21:3
Simon Peter saith unto them, I go a fishing. They say unto him, We also go with thee. They went forth and entered into a ship immediately; and that night they caught nothing.

This is the situation that many people find themselves in, they work on dead end jobs, or they raise children that don't turn out like they want; they have failed relationships, or failed investments. There are some people who end up with incurable diseases, all these situations can cause both depression and despair. Failure always comes as a surprise, except to those who expect to fail from the start. These are people who may be either insecure about themselves, or pessimistic about what they are attempting to do, or they may be simply fatalist. Either of these mind-sets will almost guarantee failure. However, for most people failure always comes unexpected, bringing along with it; unfulfilled hopes and unfulfilled potential.

Failure happens to everybody. For example, Alexander Graham Bell, the inventor of the telephone stated, *"When one door closes, another opens; but we often look so long and so regretfully upon the closed door that we do not see the one which has opened for us."* The bible puts it this way:

Revelations 3:8,
"behold I set before you an open door that no one can shut."

Failure then may either be the closing of one door, so that we can look to open another, or the ending of one chapter so that we can begin another. We must always remember that life is always filled with potential, no matter how bad things may appear. It is said that Michael Jordan was cut from his high school basketball team, while Thomas Edison was told that he was too stupid to learn, and Albert Einstein did not speak until he was four years old and did not read until he was seven. In addition, Babe Ruth made 714 home runs, but struck out 1330 times.

Failure can be the gateway to tremendous success, we must simply take the time to learn from our failures rather than be devastated by them. For example, a failure may be God's way of getting your attention.

After fishing all night and catching nothing Simon Peter and the others were in position to listen to the advice of Jesus. He met them at the point of their failure with advice on how to overcome the previously devastating night. It is at the point of failure that we are most open to hear about a better way to do what we are attempting to do.

Many people have a problem believing that God can be in bad places, however, God meets us in the wilderness situations of our lives. The wilderness is a place devoid of resources. An empty space, it is uncultivated; an inhospitable region. An unwelcoming place, a place without resources and a place with depleted means. God called Abraham to go from a place of resources to a place of depleted means in search of a blessing.

In some instances, God directs us into the wilderness, as He did with Jesus in Matthew 4, and with Israel in the book of Exodus. There are two primary things that we learn about God when we fail. First, God has integrity. He is true to his word. Second, God has awesome power.

> **Luke 5:4**
> ***Now when he had left speaking, he said unto Simon, Launch out into the deep, and let down your nets for a draught***

Jesus tells the fishermen to *"launch out into the deep."* This command suggests that failure should make us bolder, not apprehensive. However, for us to achieve this mind set we must be guided by realities that are transcendent to our present condition, or situation. We must have a since of our destiny, or our predetermined purpose.

Our destiny is that which we believe is to come, and our predetermined purpose is that which has always informed us concerning our potential. These two factors are important because they are not destroyed by the failed strategies or plans of the present. Jesus asks the men in **John 21:5**, *"**Children do you have any meat**"?* This question defines the moment. The reality here is that they had no choice other than to try again. The question is would they get bolder, or simply repeat the same failed plan that they had done the night before.

Risk should never be an issue when what we are attempting to do is essential to our very existence. Keith Webb, a life coach stated, *"in protecting ourselves from failure, we can fail to succeed."* Paul Tillich states, *"the courage to be is rooted in the God who appears when God has disappeared in the anxiety of doubt"*; and goes on to say that *"doubts are the elements of faith"*.

This idea is seen in the response of Peter:

> **Luke 5:5**
> *"**and Simon answering said unto him, Master, we have toiled all night, and have nothing; never-the-less at your word I will let down the net**."*

Peter's, never-the-less, reveals his doubt being overcome in that moment by his faith.

The example here is what Tillich is teaching us, and that is that doubt is necessary for faith, because it is in doubt that we are totally reliant on something outside of ourselves. In the case of Peter and in the case of every Christian it is the promises of God. To say never-the-less, is to admit to oneself, and to others that we are prepared to put past failures behind, and believe for the future, even though we have no certain proof that the future will be different from the past or the present. For me this is the true essence of resilient living.

For the sake of this discussion, I will list four basic things needed to maintain resilient faith;

1. **Never become a prisoner of any given moment in time**. We must always be prepared to transcend the moment. The moment is only given to us to benefit our futures, and when it is gone, that simply means that we don't need it anymore, move on.
2. **Be content with satisfying your basic needs**. Don't be greedy! This doesn't necessarily mean that you can't enjoy excess, however, it does mean that if you can't afford a Cadillac, drive a Ford, or a Jeep, or a Bug, as long as you can get from point A to point B, that is all you really need. What this means is that we can never allow our desire for more to blind us to the fact that we have enough. However, we also can never allow the fact that we have enough, to blind us to the possibility of more.
3. **We must diversify our approach to life**. Don't be one dimensional, see possibility in everyone, and everything. People who walk only on one side of the street will never know if the treasure that they seek is on the other side of the street. Jesus said, *"I must needs go through Samaria."* We should never spend our lives feeling that others are less than, or that we can do without getting to know people that are different from us. You never know who you will need to help you when the chips are down. Jesus needed a perfect stranger to help him carry the cross.

4. **Don't be absolute about anything except, your faith in God.** We must always be prepared to change our minds, and our approach. Absolute people are people who believe that their limited mind can truly comprehend absolutely the will and purposes of God for all time. Yes, we have the inspired word of God, and we see this word. Yet, many times we interpret it through the lens of our own prejudices, and cultural biases, without ever really realizing that what we are doing is in total opposition to both the love, and the grace that God has shown us. The evidence that we are on the right path is not our self- adulating piety, but rather the ultimately full, and broken nets. In **Luke 5:6** the bible states, ***"and when they had this done, they enclosed great multitude of fishes; and their nets brake."***

It is only when our nets brake, that we are put into a position to help others. This is the point of failure, it comes to teach us that just as we needed help to get us to try again, others will need that same help. When their nets broke, they called others over and began to load up their boats with the excess fish that they had caught.

What we should never do is to allow our blessing to be wasted. We waste our blessings when we continue to stuff our nets even when much of what we are catching in going to waste. This happens when we spend money on resources or things that we really don't need rather than use them to help others. This is the point of the story in the bible of the rich man in Luke 12. Rather than help the poor leper who was at his gate begging for the crumbs that fell from his table, he decided to build barns that he really didn't need.

Today many of us are doing the same thing, one rapper spent 8 million dollars on a car, rather than to use that money to help build housing for the poor people that he left behind in the projects. Abundance is not given to us to use completely on ourselves, but it is given to us to help others as well.

NOTES:

7th Principle – Use Failure as a Stepping-Stone

QUESTIONS

Dr. Jeffrey gave several examples of people who had failed miserably, ultimately; they soared to the top of their professions. Can you give other examples?

1. _____
_____
_____

2. _____
_____
_____

3. _____
_____
_____

Senario

Charley just got the gray envelop notifying her that she will not walk across the stage with the rest of her graduating class. She is embarrassed. Charley has to repeat several classes to get a diploma. That's another year of high school! Charley is ready to give up, forget about that diploma and get a job! Afterall, look at all the successful people that never graduated high school or college, and they're doing just fine … "I'll get at job; I won't have the student loans to repay." There are so many reasons for Charley to give up on her education. What 5 suggestions would you give Charley?

_____
_____

Failure should make us bolder, not apprehensive. Can you expound on this concept?

During the wilderness, Dr. Jeffrey stated that we are tempted by Pride, Purpose and Power. How does that work against this principle?

The wilderness is when God reveals His sovereignty. Please explain and give an example if this has happened to you.

We must diversify our approach to life. Don't be one dimensional. Please explain and give an example.

TRUE or FALSE

The wilderness is where you can experience God's integrity and intervention.

                True   False

When we have faith there is no room of doubt.

                True   False

We waste our blessings when we stuff our nets.

                True   False

Never become a prisoner to present time.

                True   False

SOMETHING TO PONDER

"Our destiny is that which we believe is to come, and our predetermined purpose is that which has always informed us concerning our potential ... they are not destroyed by the failed strategies or plans of the present."

"The evidence that we are on the right path is not our self- adulating piety, but rather it's our ultimately full, and broken nets."

8TH Principle

Faith Demands Synergy

Synergy can be defined as the interaction of two or more agents or forces so that their combined effect is greater than the sum of their individual effects. Cooperative interaction. The interaction of elements that when combined produce a total effect that is greater than the sum of the individual elements.

The ultimate reason for faith is to create synergy in a world filled with polarization and alienation. Beginning with the call of Abraham, leaping forward to the Ten Commandments, and reaching its crescendo with the advent of Christ, God has always called mankind to just, inter-personal relationships in order to both elevate themselves and the structures in which they exist.

The essential goal, since the fall of man has been to create a new creature, and a new world. Authentic, God-inspired human interaction is the force that is transformative enough to bring about this change.

> **1 Corinthians 12:12-18**,
>
> *"For the body is one, and hath many members, all the member of that one body, being many, are one body; so also is Christ. For by one Spirit are we all baptized into one body, whether we be bond or free, and have been all made to drink into one Spirit, for the body is not one member, but many."*

This text goes on to require that we accept our differences, and create by our coming together, the oneness that is God's will for the human family.

In the book of Ezekiel when God tells Ezekiel to prophesy to the bones, He defines the nature and character of our 'Faith' mission today. Our job is to speak to the divisions of our time in order to bring men to a place where they understand and appreciate their need for each other. This the difference between the ethic of Dr. King, and the new age gospel of self-aspiration. Although faith includes self-aspiration, and self-renewal, our faith makes it clear that "I am my brother's keeper!" In the story of the Good Samaritan, Jesus makes it clear that I am required to be a good neighbor.

One of the true obstacles to synergy, or inter-personal harmony is 'lack'.

Matthew 14:13-21

When Jesus heard what had happened, he withdrew by boat privately to a solitary place. Hearing of this, the crowds followed him on foot from the towns. When Jesus landed and saw a large crowd, he had compassion on them and healed their sick. As evening approached, the disciples came to him and said, "This is a remote place, and it's already getting late. Send the crowds away, so they can go to the villages and buy themselves some food." Jesus replied, "They do not need to go away. You give them something to eat." "We have here only five loaves of bread and two fish," they answered. "Bring them here to me," he said. And he directed the people to sit down on the grass. Taking the five loaves and the two fish and looking up to heaven, he gave thanks and broke the loaves. Then he gave them to the disciples, and the disciples gave them to the people. They all ate and were satisfied, and the disciples picked up twelve basketfuls of broken pieces that were left over. The number of those who ate was about five thousand men, besides women and children.

The bible tells the story of Jesus feeding the five thousand. One of the points in this story is that lack interrupts ministry. It creates tension between our spiritual and physical needs. It does this because lack affects our health, it affects our social opportunities, lack can kill, it can cause abuse, or lead to crime. With this in mind, it is no wonder that Jesus felt it was necessary to address the situation, contrary to the response of His disciples who felt that the lack of the people was not their responsibility. In verse 15 they are quoted as saying, *"this is a remote place, and it's already getting late. Send the crowds away so they can go to the villages and buy themselves some food."* There is a story that is told about how to deal with the hopelessness caused by collective lack.

> *A kindly, old stranger was walking through the land when he came upon a village. As he entered, the villagers moved towards their homes locking doors and windows.*
>
> *The stranger smiled and asked, why are you all so frightened? I am a simple traveler, looking for a soft place to stay for the night and a warm place for a meal.*
>
> *"There's not a bite in the whole province," he was told. We are weak and our children are starving. Better keep moving."*
>
> *"Oh, I have everything I need," he said. "In fact, I was thinking of making some stone soup to share with all of you."*
>
> *He pulled an iron cauldron from his cloak, filled it with water, and began to build a fire under it. Then with great ceremony, he drew an ordinary-looking stone from a silken bag and dropped it into the water.*
>
> *By now, hearing the rumor of food, most of the villagers had come out of their homes or watched from their windows. As the stranger sniffed the 'broth' and licked his lips in anticipation, hunger began to overcome their fear.*
>
> *"Ahhhhh" the stranger said to himself rather loudly, "I do like a tasty stone soup. Of course stone soup with cabbage ... that's hard to beat."*
>
> *Soon a villager approached hesitantly, holding a small cabbage he'd retrieved from its hiding place, and added it to pot.*
>
> *"Wonderful!" cried the stranger. "You know, I once had stone soup with cabbage and a bit of salt beef as well, and it was fit for a king."*

The village butcher managed to find some salt beef ... And so it went, through potatoes, onions, carrots, mushrooms, and so on, until there was indeed a delicious meal for everyone in the village to share.

The village elder offered the stranger a great deal of money for the magical stone, but he refused to sell it and traveled on the next day.

As he left, the stranger came upon a group of village children standing near the road. He gave the silken bag containing the stone to the youngest child, whispering to a group,

"It was not the stone, but the villagers that had performed the magic." unknown

The moral of this story is that sowing into situations of lack, is contagious. Our goal must never be to simply promote our own selfish interest. The call of God is that we hear as well, the collective call of those who may be isolated in a desert place.

The natural response to 'lack' is the response of the disciples, "Send them away," however faith is never practiced on the isolated island of indifference. This is the lesson that the rich young ruler learned when Jesus told him to *"sell all that he had and give the money to the poor, and then come follow Him."*

Indifference, in the wake of hurting people; is not the testimony that 'authentic' faith compels us to practice. Send them away raises the question; 'Who are those who must be sent away'? It suggests that some people deserve to be fed while others are left to fend for themselves.

The first point of this story is that God creates capacity with whatever we surrender to him. In **Luke 6:9** the bible states, **"there is a lad here, which hath five barley loaves and two small fishes but what are they among so many."**

True abundance is only created when we sow into the lack of others. The lad represents our willingness to surrender our resources to the will of God in order to be a blessing for others. The disciples represent the natural inclination to see your resources as inadequate to meet the needs of the situation. There are many who will never see increase because of their unwillingness to surrender their little to the cause of the many.

Today in the African American community we spend over one trillion dollars a year in this economy, however we have a collective poverty rate of 27.4% for adults, and 45.8% for children, this is because lads are not giving their lunch for the good of those who are languishing in lack. Some might ask the question, what does this have to do with my personal increase? The issue here is that personal increase alone is never going to be enough to satisfy the call of God for us to also be good neighbors. Send them away is never acceptable to Jesus Christ, it only creates broken people.

There are three primary ways that we can become that lad;

1. We can become that lad through our tithes. The bible says in **Malachi 3:10** states, ***"bring the whole tithe into the store house that there may be food in my house prove me says the Lord almighty and see if I will not throw open the floodgates of heaven and pour out so much blessing that there will not be room enough to store it."***

2. We can become like the good Samaritan and always be available to help those who are in peril,

3. We can be like Jesus and understand that our sacrifice will ultimately lead to human redemption.

In situations of lack, faith demands cooperation, we must learn that lack is the common denominator that unites us all. What your brother is not, you are; and what you are not, your brother or sister is. We don't know this until we sit down in companies, in groups, in churches and in community centers. When we sit together, we realize that together we have enough for everybody. Because if you give your loaves and two fish, I'm sure that somebody else also brought their lunch.

Authentic synergy is satisfying. The bible says that they were filled. They were satisfied. They had a fulfillment of both their spiritual and physical expectations, wishes and needs. This to me is the definition of abundance, not just personal wealth or selfish and pretentious concerns, but satisfaction for the whole.

Not only were they filled, but they had leftovers.

NOTES:

8TH Principle – Faith Demands Synergy

QUESTIONS

Can you give an example of Synergy?

_____
_____
_____
_____
_____

What the fundamental goal of God for mankind and what will it take?

_____
_____
_____
_____

Dr. Jeffrey states God uses mankind to created synergy to both elevate ourselves and the structure in which we exist. Please expound on this concept.

_____
_____
_____
_____
_____

Why "Faith" can never become isolated?

_____
_____
_____
_____
_____
_____
_____
_____

Match the Phrase

A. In situations of lack   ____ Your brother's keeper

B. Faith   ____ As thyself

C. The true enemy of Synergy   ____ Demands cooperation

D. Love thy neighbor   ____ That unites us all

E. What your brother is not   ____ Creates synergy

F. You are   ____ Miracles can happen

G. Natural response to Lack   ____ You are

H. By working together   ____ Lack

I. Lack is the common denominator   ____ To send away

TRUE or FALSE

Personal increase is never enough to be good neighbors.

       True   False

Lack is a common denominator that unites us all.

       True   False

You are not my Keeper.

       True   False

Authentic Synergy is can never truly satisfy.

       True   False

God creates capacity with whatever we surrender to Him.

       True   False

Something to Ponder

True abundance is only created when we sow into the lack of others

9ᵀᴴ Principle

Stay Healthy

Defining purpose for the body:

> **1 Corinthians 6:20**
>
> ***Do you not know that you are the temple of God and that the Spirit of God dwells in you? If anyone defiles the temple of God, God will destroy him. For the temple of God is holy, which temple you are.***

Do you perceive with your eyes, or senses, notice, pay attention, cherish ... This is information that you cannot ignore.

> *You are* – second person plural of "to be". You have been, or become, to belong to. This statement is without qualifications. *You are* – You use to be lost creatures, but now "You are" ... have become, been brought with a price. You must recognize, open your eyes to this fact, that your bodies are temples.

Temples may be shrines, often stately or sumptuous, enclosing the remains of relics of saints or other holy persons. In the case of Christians, we embody the Holy Spirit. Temples are also for religious inspiration, hallowed places, receptacles for sacred things. As Christians we have been redeemed to become temples.

Therefore, we should honor and respect our bodies, and this means that we should honor and respect both what we put into our bodies and what we do with our bodies. According to the department of Health and Human Services, 5% of adults participate in a minimum of 30 minutes of physical activity each day. This report also states that only 35-44% of adults 75 years or older are physically active, in addition only 34% of adults 65-74 are physically active. According to this report 80% of all adults do not meet guidelines of being healthy. However, this may be because 80.2 million people in this country age six and older are physically inactive. The report states that we eat less than the recommended amounts of vegetables, fruits, whole-grains and dairy than we should. We also eat too much sodium, 90% of us eat more sodium than is recommended.

It becomes clear as we look at these statistics that the church needs to do more to teach about our responsibility to be healthy citizens of the kingdom. First, we must emphasize the fact that healthy living is just as important as spiritual living.

The bible tells us in **1 Corinthians 6**, that the "***temple of God is holy, which temple we are***". A fundamental part of living holy is eating holy and treating our bodies as holy vessels. It is believed that a general goal is for us to exercise at least 30 minutes a day, or 300 minutes a week for maximum effect. In addition. it is believed that a good diet is low in fat, cholesterol, sodium and sugar; and high in vegetables, fruits, beans, nuts and whole-grain, this however may not always be possible for many poor Christians trapped in food deserts.

There are approximately 2.3 million Americans including 6.5 million children living in food deserts in this country; these are areas that are more than a mile away from supermarkets. Our mission is two-fold, first we must see our own bodies as temples, and then we must see others through the same lens. The body then becomes a visible testimony to our spiritual walk, as it relates to how we treat our own bodies, and how we feel responsibility towards the bodies of others who are less fortunate.

Daniel 1:8

"but Daniel purposed in his heart that he would not defile himself with the portion of the kings meat, not with the wine which he drank; therefore he requested of the Prince of the eunuchs that he might not defile himself."

The message in this verse is that our choice of food separates us from those who would eat the king's meat. Daniel in this text calls for us to be careful about our diets, so that we can be the living testimony that we are called on to be. Today much of the food that we eat is not healthy because of pesticides, and organic biopesticides that have become a part of our food chain. These pesticides have a harmful health effect on our bodies, and in children.

Accidental exposures to high levels of pesticides are associated with childhood cancers, attention deficit, hyperactivity disorder (ADHD) and autism.

Food however is not the only thing that we should be concerned about, by some estimates, approximately 40% of all deaths in the United States are premature, at least 900,000 deaths annually according to David Anderson Ph.D., StayWell Health Management. These deaths are due to unhealthy lifestyle choices such as tobacco use, poor diet, sedentary lifestyle, misuse of alcohol and drugs, and accidents.

As we seek to live healthier lives, we must always remember that God's work in this world is done through us.

> **Romans 12:1-2**
>
> *"I beseech you therefore, brethren, by the mercies of God, that you present your bodies a living sacrifice, holy, acceptable unto God, which is your reasonable service. And be not conformed to this world; but be ye transformed by the renewing of your mind, that you may prove what is that good, and acceptable, and perfect, will of God."*

This is the mind-set that Daniel had even in captivity in Babylon. He committed himself, body, mind and soul to the task of being a living example. However, as Daniel teaches us it is not always easy to be a living example. In Daniel's case he was put into a position where he had to choose between his life- style and the life- style of the people of Babylon. Daniel chose to be true to himself and his God. His choice however led to him being persecuted. Our choices today may not lead us to be persecuted by others, but it may lead to us having serious internal struggles with ourselves.

The King in this story of Daniel, represents that which tempts us to betray our commitments, or to abandon our God-inspired practices. In every struggle there will always be the king, the one who is greater than we are, that power that compels us to abandon our course, to give in to our urges, to abdicate our promises to both God and to ourselves. The King represent that which tempts us to be like everybody else, rather than seeking to be the temple of God.

We bring the king under subjection simply by continuing to do what is right, even in the face of great peril. This peril can be either imagined or real, but we know that it is peril because it forces us to decide, or to choose. Daniel chose to stay the course and was subsequently put into a den of lions.

The den of lions represents the penalty that the world or the flesh places upon us because of our decision to pursue the way led by God, rather than to change our minds and simply become like everybody else. Daniel survived the den of lions, and so can we. He survived because of God's intervention,

> **Daniel 6:22**
>
> ***"My God hath sent his angel, and hath shut the lion's mouths, and they have not hurt me; forasmuch as before him innocence was found in me; and also before thee".***

This is the assurance that we all have when we seek to do the right thing. Committing yourself to seeing your body as the temple of God, most likely will not lead to you being put into a literal lion's den, however, it may not be an easy walk for you when it comes to breaking old habits and casting off old demons that are destroying your health. Therefore, it is important for us to remember how Daniel won his victory.

1. **He was serious about Prayer**. If we are to be the temple of God, we also must be serious about prayer.
2. **This involves being serious about Worship.** Worship is an important component of prayer. Worship can be defined as the loving expression of praise to God for what He is and His ways.
3. **It also involves Thanksgiving**
    > **Matthew 11:25:** ***"At that time Jesus answered and said, I thank thee, O Father, Lord of heaven and earth, because thou hast hid these things from the wise and prudent, and hast revealed them unto babes,"***

> **John 11:41:** *"Then they took away the stone from the place where the dead was laid. And Jesus lifted up his eyes, and said, Father, I thank thee that thou hast heard me."*

4. **As well as Confession**

> **1 Kings 8:47:** *Yet if they shall bethink themselves in the land whither they were carried captives, and repent, and make supplication unto thee in the land of them that carried them captives, saying, We have sinned, and have done perversely, we have committed wickedness;*

5. **We must not worry about the opinions of others**.

> **Daniel 6:10** *"Now when Daniel knew that the writing was signed, he went into his house; and his windows being open in his chamber toward Jerusalem, he kneeled upon his knees three times a day, and prayed and gave thanks before his God, as he did aforetime."*

Daniel was so committed to his course of action that he was resolute in the face of opposition and differing opinions. We also must be able to turn off the outside noise that would prevent us from doing and being all that we desire to become.

There is an old Aesop Fable that states:

> *"A man and his son were once going with their Donkey to market. As they were walking along by its side a countryman passed them and said; "you fools, what is a Donkey for but to ride upon?" So, the man put the boy on the donkey and they went on their way, but soon they passed a group of men, one of whom said; "see that lazy youngster, he lets his father walk while he rides." So, the man ordered his boy to get off and got on himself, but they hadn't gone far when they passed two women, one of whom said to the other; "shame on that lazy lout let his poor little son trudge along." Well, the man didn't know what to do, but at last he took his boy up before him on the donkey. By this time they had come to the town, and the passers-by began to jeer and point at them. The man stopped and asked what they were scoffing at. The men said; "aren't you ashamed of yourself for overloading that poor donkey of yours—you and your hulking son?" The man and boy got off and tried to think what to do. They thought and*

they thought, till at last they cut down a pole, tied the donkey's feet to it, and raised the pole and the donkey to their shoulders. They went along amid the laughter of all who met them till they came to market bridge, when the donkey, getting one of his feet loose, kicked out and caused the boy to drop his end of the pole. In the struggle the donkey fell over the bridge, and his fore-feet being tied together he was drowned. "That will teach you," said the old man who had followed them:"

Today, we live in a world where many don't want to suffer, or to go through any difficulty. Not only did Daniel practice prayer, and not only did he not allow the opinions of others to change his mind, he also endured the lions den. However, this is why Paul tells Timothy to endure hardship.

2 Timothy 2:3-7

"thou therefore endure hardness, as a good soldier of Jesus Christ. No man that wars entangles himself with the affairs of this life; that he may please him who hath chosen him to be a soldier."

NOTES

9th Principle – Stay Healthy

QUESTIONS

After studying the 9th Principle we find that our Spiritual health is just as important as our Physical health. How do they support each other in regard to your Temple?.

_____
_____
_____
_____
_____
_____
_____

Dr. Jeffrey stated our mission pertaining to our spiritual health is two-fold. Can you explain this concept and as Christians, what we must do?

_____
_____
_____
_____
_____
_____
_____

Name 3 behavioral changes you can make that will be your "Reasonable" service whereas you can present your body as a "Living Sacrifice"?

1. _____
_____
_____

2. _____
_____
_____

3. _____
_____
_____

In the 9th Principle, the King is represented as that which tempts us to betray our commitments. Today what does that looks like and what are some of the perils that we may face as a result?

_____
_____
_____
_____
_____
_____
_____

How was Daniel victorious?

_____
_____
_____
_____
_____
_____
_____
_____
_____

Something to Ponder

"Eat your food as your medicine, otherwise you will have to eat medicines as your food." Dr. Michael Osae made this statement at the World Biodiversity Day celebration, held at the Academy of Arts and Sciences auditorium in Accra, on May 22, 2019.

In your own words, explain this scripture.

> ***"I beseech you therefore, brethren, by the mercies of God, that you present your bodies a living sacrifice, holy, acceptable unto God, which is your reasonable service. And be not conformed to this world; but be ye transformed by the renewing of your mind, that you may prove what is that good, and acceptable, and perfect, will of God."***

_____

_____

_____

_____

_____

_____

_____

_____

_____

_____

_____

_____

10th Principle

It's A Matter of Time

According to the Greeks, there are two ways in which 'time' impacts our lives, the two ways are Chronos, and Kairos.

> **Chronos** is what we call chronological time, which is the indefinite continued progress of existence and events in the past, present and future.

Chronos is the means by which we frame history, and our lives. It is time measured in hours, days and minutes, even seconds when it comes to some athletic events. It is in time that we plan, or schedule activities.

It is this time that we give meaning to all process and activity. For example, we divide our human development into eight primary stages, infant, toddlers, early childhood, school age, adolescence, young adulthood, adulthood, and old age. Each of these stages are measured by time. We do the same things in our workplaces, in our athletic activities, and in our everyday lives. We eat breakfast in the morning, we eat lunch around noon, we eat dinner in the afternoon or early evening.

However as Christian; although we are similarly positioned in time, we also have an appreciation for the revelatory time of God, embodied in the notion of Kairos time.

> **Kairos** time means the right time or the opportune time.

This notion of Kairos is not allowed for in Chronos time, a thing either comes on time or it is late, and in some instances too late. Kairos time holds out the belief that what may seem late or too late in Chronos time, may simply be waiting for the opportune time.

The notion of the supreme moment, the right time is a transcendent notion, because it calls us to the fact that there are some things that we can't predict, or schedule. There are some things that we simply have to wait in a timeless space to achieve or receive. For example,

African people were in slavery for 250 years, and then the moment came, and we were set free. We knew that moment was coming, as evidenced by our songs, *"Soon I will be done with the troubles of the world"*, or *"Go down Moses way down in Egypt land, tell old Pharaoh to let my people go"*, or even more poignant, *"I'm so glad trouble don't last always oh my lord, oh my lord, what shall I do"*. These songs illustrate that we knew that freedom from slavery was coming, we just couldn't put a time on our expectation.

It is at the point that we are unable to put a time constraint on our human expectations that we enter Kairos time. The existence of Kairos time is the substance of our faith and the bases of our hope.

> In the midst of the civil rights struggle, Dr. Martin Luther King expressed this best when he said, *"we've got some difficult days ahead. But it really doesn't matter with me now because I've been to the mountaintop…I've looked over and I've seen the promised land. I may not get there with you. But I want you to know tonight that we as a people will get to the promised land."*
>
> **Romans 8:24-25**,
>
> **"for we are saved by hope; but hope that is seen is not hope; for what a man sees why does he yet hope? But if we hope for that we see not, then do we with patience wait for it."**

This is the bases on which Abraham waited until he was 100 years old to father a child, or Job persevered after losing everything only to say, "In all my appointed time, I will wait until my change comes."

First, we must accept the fact that Chronos time is not our friend, and will not always present to us manageable situations, or time to resolve problems that defy a given space of time.

In 1 Samuel 13, Saul the king of Israel finds himself in a situation where time is not on his side. The prophet Samuel had instructed him to wait for seven days, and then Samuel would come and offer an offering to God for victory over the Philistines, however in the interim the Philistines gathered to engage in an imminent attack on the forces of Saul.

1 Samuel 13:5

"and the Philistines gathered themselves together to fight with Israel, thirty thousand chariots, and six thousand horsemen, and people as the sand which is on the sea shore in multitude; and they came up, and pitched in Michmash, eastward from Bethaven."

King Saul was facing an overwhelming force, and time was not on his side.

There are many times when we are put in situations where the demand is greater than our present resources. It is in these moments that we are called upon to practice a resolute faith.

A resolute faith is one that will allow us to say that this moment in time will not define the ultimate outcome for my life. Saul had the promise of Samuel that he would return in seven days and seek God's help in defeating the Philistines, however that was eventually not enough for Saul. Like Saul there will be many times in our lives when we will have to simply depend and trust in the promises of God for our lives.

As we later understand in the text, seven days did not mean literally seven days, it meant at the right time, at God's appointed time. The lesson that we must learn here is that God will never allow Himself to become a prisoner to our time schedule or our perceived needs at a certain time in our lives. What we are always called to do, is to wait on God's time.

We know that we are not waiting on God's time, when our actions, or activities are guided by fear.

1 Samuel 13:6-7

"when the men of Israel saw that they were in a strait, (for the people were distressed,) then the people did hide themselves in caves, and in thickets, and in rocks, and in high places, and in pits. An some of the Hebrews went over Jordan to the land of Gad and Gilead. As for Saul, he was yet in Gilgal, and all the people followed him trembling."

These verses describe panic, that ran from the King on down to his people. Panic will cause you to hide.

They hid in thickets, they hid in the rocks, they even hid in holes in the ground. We always know when we are hiding, because we are in places that we would never be except for the fact that we are afraid; we are with people that we would never be with, we make decisions that we would never make, if it were not for the fact that we are afraid.

2 Timothy 1:7

"for the Spirit God gave us does not make us timid, or afraid, but gives us power, love and self-discipline."

We can never allow a moment in time to cause us to panic and hide from our walk in this world. The enemies that the Hebrews faced were as the "sand on the seashore." Maybe this is the kind of situation that you may face, however, we must hold on in these moments to the promises of God as expressed in Philippians 4:13.

Philippians 4:13

"I can do all things through Christ who gives me strength."

Don't yield to the temptation to hide, or to run just because you may feel overwhelmed. Oscar Wilde an Irish poet and playwright put it this way, *"actors are so fortunate. They can choose whether they will appear in tragedy or in comedy, whether they will suffer or make merry, laugh or shed tears. But in real life it is different. Most men and women are forced to perform parts for which they have no qualifications. Our Guildenstern's play Hamlet for us, and our Hamlets have to jest like Prince Hal. The world is a stage, but the play is badly cast."*

Guildenstern is a character in a comedy, and Prince Hal refers to a standard term used in literary criticism to refer to Shakespeare's portrayal of the young Henry V of England as a prince before his accession to the throne. In other words, most; if not all of us, must play in roles of life which we are not qualified to play, but forced to do so because of the circumstances in which we find ourselves.

The warning in this text is that we should never seek to take control of God's time. The act or action of God, in time, is completely outside of our ability to control.

1 Samuel 13:8-12

"and he tarried seven days, according to the set time that Samuel had appointed; but Samuel came not to Gilgal; and the people scattered from him. And Saul said, bring here a burnt offering to me, and peace offerings and he offered the burnt offering. And it came to pass, that as soon as he had made an end of offering the burnt offering, behold, Samuel came."

According to this text Saul got tired of waiting, and so he took matters into his own hands. This is what we cannot do, because to do so is to make ourselves god by putting our own needs and desires before the will and plan of God. It is not always easy to wait on God, but that is exactly what we are required to do.

The consequence for not waiting is to lose God's intended blessing.

1 Samuel 13:13-14

"and Samuel said to Saul, you have done foolishly; you have not kept the commandment of the Lord your God, which he commanded you; for now would the Lord have established your kingdom upon Israel forever. But now your kingdom shall not continue; the Lord hath sought him a man after his own heart, and the Lord hath commanded him to be captain over his people, because you have not kept that which the Lord commanded you."

Saul not only messed things up for himself, but for his descendants as well. When we take matters into our own hands simply because we can't wait on God to move with us, we put everything in jeopardy, our families, our jobs, our dreams, our hopes, our children and grandchildren, everything.

Isaiah 40:31

"but they that wait upon the Lord shall renew their strength; they shall mount up with wings as eagles; they shall run, and not be weary; and they shall walk, and not faint."

Always remember it's a matter of time.

NOTES

_____
_____
_____
_____
_____
_____
_____
_____
_____
_____
_____
_____
_____
_____
_____
_____
_____

10th Principle – It's a Matter of Time

QUESTIONS

Describe an event that happened in Kairos time.

_____
_____
_____
_____
_____
_____
_____
_____

Why does Dr. Jeffrey state that Chronos time is not our friend? Give an example.

_____
_____
_____
_____
_____
_____
_____

At what point, as Christians, do we enter into Kairos time? What are some of the manifestations?

_____

_____

_____

_____

_____

_____

The 10th Principle teaches us that the consequence for not waiting on God's timing is to lose God's intended blessing. Have there been times in your life when you should have waited on God's Timing? Please explain.

_____

_____

_____

_____

_____

_____

_____

_____

Can you describe Resolute Faith and give an example?

_____

_____

_____

_____

Match the Phrases

A. I can do all things   ____ of Time

B. For hope that is seen   ____ through Christ that strengthens me

C. They shall mount up with wings   ____ evidence of things not seen

D. Soon I will be done   ____ is not timid nor afraid

E. It's a matter   ____ is not hope

F. I will never leave thee   ____ with the troubles of the world

G. For the spirit God gave us   ____ as eagles

H. Faith   ____ Nor forsake thee

Something to Ponder

"but they that wait upon the Lord shall renew their strength; they shall mount up with wings as eagles; they shall run, and not be weary; and they shall walk, and not faint."

We know that we are not waiting on God's time, when our actions, or activities are guided by fear.

11th Principle

It's Never Too Late

The story of Samson at its core is a story of how a man born with a Godly purpose and mission allowed himself to become distracted, and nearly destroyed by the very people that he was born to defeat and defend his people against.

Judges 13

*And the children of Israel did evil again in the sight of the L*ORD*; and the L*ORD *delivered them into the hand of the Philistines forty years. And there was a certain man of Zorah, of the family of the Danites, whose name was Manoah; and his wife was barren, and bare not. And the angel of the L*ORD *appeared unto the woman, and said unto her, Behold now, thou art barren, and bearest not: but thou shalt conceive, and bear a son. Now therefore beware, I pray thee, and drink not wine nor strong drink, and eat not any unclean thing: For, lo, thou shalt conceive, and bear a son; and no razor shall come on his head: for the child shall be a Nazarite unto God from the womb: and he shall begin to deliver Israel out of the hand of the Philistines. Then the woman came and told her husband, saying, A man of God came unto me, and his countenance was like the countenance of an angel of God, very terrible: but I asked him not whence he was, neither told he me his name: But he said unto me, Behold, thou shalt conceive, and bear a son; and now drink no wine nor strong drink, neither eat any unclean thing: for the child shall be a Nazarite to God from the womb to the day of his death.*[8] *Then Manoah intreated the L*ORD*, and said, O my Lord, let the man of God which thou didst send come again unto us, and teach us what we shall do unto the child that shall be born. And God hearkened to the voice of Manoah; and the angel of God came again unto the woman as she sat in the field: but Manoah her husband was not with her. And the woman made haste, and ran, and shewed her husband, and said unto him, Behold, the man hath appeared unto me, that came unto me the other day. And Manoah arose, and went after his wife, and came to the man, and said unto him, Art thou the man that spakest unto the woman? And he said, I am. And Manoah said, Now let thy words come* *to pass. How shall we order the child, and how shall we do unto him? And the angel of the LORD said unto Manoah, Of all that I said unto the woman let her beware. She may not eat of any thing that cometh of the vine, neither let her drink wine or strong drink, nor eat any unclean thing: all that I commanded her let her observe. And Manoah said unto the angel of the LORD, I pray thee, let us detain thee, until we shall have made ready a kid for thee. And the angel of the LORD said unto Manoah, Though thou detain me, I will not eat of thy bread: and if thou wilt offer a burnt offering, thou must offer it unto the LORD. For Manoah knew not that he was an angel of the LORD. And Manoah said unto the angel of the LORD, What is thy name, that when thy sayings come to pass we may do thee honour? And the angel of the LORD said unto him, Why askest thou thus after my name, seeing it is secret? So Manoah took a kid with a meat offering, and offered it upon a rock unto the LORD: and the angel did wonderously; and Manoah and his wife looked on. For it came to pass, when the flame went up toward heaven from off the altar, that the angel of the LORD ascended in the flame of the altar. And Manoah and his wife looked on it, and fell on their faces to the ground. But the angel of the LORD did no more appear to Manoah and to his wife. Then Manoah knew that he was an angel of the LORD. And Manoah said unto his wife, We shall surely die, because we have seen God. But his wife said unto him, If the LORD were pleased to kill us, he would not have received a burnt offering and a meat offering at our hands, neither would he have shewed us all these things, nor would as at this time have told us such things as these. And the woman bare a son, and called his name Samson: and the child grew, and the LORD blessed him. And the Spirit of the LORD began to move him at times in the camp of Dan between Zorah and Eshtaol.*

Samson's parents, Manoah and his wife could not have children because his wife was barren. Because of her barrenness God sent an angel to Manoah's wife, and the angel promises her that she will bear a son. However, the promise comes with conditions; she is told not to contaminate her body with any alcohol, because her child will be a Nazarite. In other words, God intends for Samson to be dedicated to God from the time of his birth. The angel also told her that her son would save the Israelites from the Philistines.

The Philistines had come in and conquered Israel, they took away their swords and spears so that they could not fight; and they robbed their land of all the crops, and the people suffered because there was not enough food, and many died of starvation.

Moreover, the promise of a child to Manoah and his wife also came with a condition for the unborn child. They were told that when Samson grew up that he would save Israel from the Philistines. However, they were also told that he should never drink any wine or strong drink, for as long as he lived. In addition, they were told that his hair should be allowed to grow long and should never be cut, **"for he shall be a Nazarite under a vow to the Lord"**.

> It was the custom of Israel that when a child was given especially to God, or when a man gave himself to some work for God, he was forbidden to drink wine, and as a sign, his hair was left to grow long while the vow or promise to God was upon him. People who took these vows were called Nazarites, which means "one who has a vow".

Samson grew to become the strongest man alive, and because of his strength he began the process of setting his people free, not by raising an army, but by simply using his own strength.

Samson in many ways personifies what can happen to those of us who are empowered with the plan and the purpose of God; and seeks to carry out that plan and purpose in the world.

Like Samson, through Christ Jesus we are also given great strength and purpose in this world. When we are born into the Kingdom of God, we are born as Samson was born to do spiritual warfare against the enemies of God that seek to hold the children of God captive to their schemes and devices. We are born again, both to do battle and to walk in the strength and power of the might of Christ. However, many times we find ourselves weakened and overwhelmed by the powers of this world, in the same way that Samson found himself bound and subservient to the Philistines.

Samson's problems began when he became enticed by the women of the people that he was sworn to fight on behalf of his people. Great strength many times leads us to believe that we are impervious to the carnal things of this world. We may feel that because of God's grace, we can get away with things that might destroy other people. This religious arrogance that is fueled by our understanding both of God's purpose for our lives, and God's abiding grace towards us has led many Christians, and churches to a disastrous end.

2 Corinthians 6:16-17

"and what agreement has the temple of God with idols? For you are the temple of the living God; as God hath said, I will dwell in them, and walk in them; and I will be their God, and they shall be my people. Wherefore, come our from among them, and be you separate, says the Lord, and touch not the unclean thing; and I will receive you."

What the writer is saying here is not that we should have no dealings with the world that we have come to do battle with, he is saying that we should not as Paul puts in his letter to Timothy, "**don't become entangled with the affairs of this world**."

The notion of entanglement simply means that we should never allow ourselves to become dependent on anything that is against God, and the will and purposes of God for our lives. Samson did this on two occasions, and the last time that he did it, he was taken captive.

There will always be things in this life that will seek to compel us to betray our purpose, or compromise our commitment to the cause of Jesus Christ, but we can never allow ourselves to become so dependent on these things that we put their needs or request before our purpose and our promise to God.

In the story, Samson gave himself completely over to Delilah, to the extent that he betrayed both his purpose and his vows to God, and because of this, he lost his power to defeat the enemy.

Judges 16:20

"He awoke, and rose up, expecting to find himself strong as before; for he did not at first know that his long hair had been cut off. But the vow to the Lord was broken, and the Lord had left him. He was now as weak as other men, and as helpless in the hands of his enemies as others"

There are two primary things that the world does to the people of God who lose their power, they blind them and they bind them. This is what they did to Samson.

When we become blind, we become unable to see our purpose, or to see the hand of God in our lives, we are left all alone. When we become blind, we are no longer able to notice, understand or judge our own behavior or the behavior of those that are around us. When we become blind certain information is concealed or withheld intentionally, and we can't see to tell the difference. When we become blind, our lives are no longer controlled by the Spirit, but rather by our own blind destiny.

They bound him also, so that he could no longer do for himself, but rather was dependent on them to do for him. They made him accountable to them, answerable to them, they forced him to grind their corn. They obligated him to their needs, they became a replacement for the vows that he had made to God. They made him into a beast to carry their burden.

Judges 16:21-24,

"but the Philistines took him, and put out his eyes, and brought him down to Gaza, and bound him with fetters of brass; and he did grind in the prison house. Howbeit the hair of his head began to grow again after he was shaven. Then the lords of the Philistines gathered them together for to offer a great sacrifice unto Dagon their god, and to rejoice; for they said, our god hath delivered Samson our enemy into our hand." The redemptive part of this story is that Samson renewed his vows to the Lord. Redemption can be defined as "the act of saving or being saved from sin, error or evil." It is also "the act of regaining possession of something in exchange for payment or clearing of a debt."

Samson's redemption was different from ours because Samson paid the price for his redemption by dying with the Philistines. For us as Christians the price has already been paid. As Christians we believe that Jesus Christ through his sacrificial death purchased us from the slavery of our sins and set us free from the bondage that came as a result of that sin.

There are two Greek words that relate to the Christian understanding of redemption, the first is "Exagorazo". This word involves going from something to something else. For us as Christians it means Christ freeing us from the bondage of the law and giving us freedom to have a new life in him. Another Greek word connected with redemption is 'Lutroo', which means to obtain release by the payment of a price. The price for us as Christians was Christ's precious blood, which obtained our release from sin and death.

As in the case of Samson, God always gives us an opportunity to demonstrate our redemption to an unbelieving world.

2 Corinthians 4:2

"but by manifestation of the truth commending ourselves to every man's conscience in the sight of God."

As believers God empowers us to manifest His power that is in us because of our redemption. It is this manifestation that testifies to the world that we are renewed, changed, and set apart to do a different more powerful work than before.

Judges 16:30

"so the dead which he slew at his death were more than they which he slew in his life."

The change that happens to us after our redemption increases our capacity. It is this increase in capacity that allows us to personify the new creatures that we are made into through our having been redeemed.

One day there was a great feast held by the Philistines in the temple of their fish-god, Dagon. The temple was filled with people, there were more than three thousand men and women in the temple. They sent for Samson, so that they could revel in the power of their God. Samson came into the temple led by a little boy. He said to the boy **"take me up to the front of the temple, so that I may stand by one of the pillars and lean against it."** The bible tells us that Samson then began to pray, **"O Lord God, remember me, I pray thee and give me**

strength." After praying he then placed his hands on the pillars and pushed them in order to cause the building to collapse.

The ultimate point of this story is that it is truly never too late to leap into your purpose. God will always give us another chance when we are repentant, it doesn't matter how old you are, or what you have done in your life, you can still accomplish the desires of your heart, whether it's going back to school, or starting your own business, or making peace with your estranged father, or mother, or siblings. It is never too late!

God through Jesus Christ has atoned for your sins, you are a new creature, therefore always resist any notion that would give yourself over to the valley of regret and hopelessness. God has come to give you New Hope.

NOTES

_____
_____
_____
_____
_____
_____
_____
_____
_____
_____

11th Principle – It's Never too Late

QUESTIONS

The story of Samson describes how we as Christians can be thrown off our mission when we mingle with the world. List the two things that happens and please give an example.

_____
_____
_____
_____
_____
_____
_____

What were the conditions to become a Nazarite?

_____
_____
_____
_____
_____
_____

Dr. Jeffrey uses the metaphor of the story of Samson as it relates to our Christian journey. Can you list some of the comparisons?

_____

_____

_____

_____

_____

_____

When we are empowered or called to do great things, we may believe that we are protected from the carnal things of this world. How is that possible and Why?

_____

_____

_____

_____

_____

_____

_____

Explain "Redemption"

_____

_____

Why was Samson's redemption different from today's Christian experience?

Dr. Jeffrey gave an example of Samson as it refers to the 11th Principle, "It's Never too Late." Can you give another example referencing today's society to your personal journey?

Match the Phrases

A. Exagorazo   ____ with the affairs of the world

B. Don't become entangled   ____ from one thing to something else

C. When we become blind   ____ to obtain release by the payment

D. Redemption   ____ God will give us another chance

E. Lutroo   ____ no longer controlled by the Spirit

F. When we repent   ____ saved from sin, error, or evil

Something to Ponder

"There will always be things in this life that will seek to compel us to betray our purpose, or our commitment or have us compromise our cause of service to Jesus Christ, but we can never allow ourselves to become so dependent on these things until we put their needs or request before our purpose and our promise to God."

www.ingramcontent.com/pod-product-compliance
Lightning Source LLC
Chambersburg PA
CBHW080517110426
42742CB00017B/3148